IPPFA
Retirement Guide

UPDATED FOR 2025

IPPFA RETIREMENT GUIDE

(3RD EDITION)

ILLINOIS PUBLIC PENSION FUND ASSOCIATION

FOREWORD BY
JAMES MCNAMEE
PRESIDENT

WINDY CITY PUBLISHERS

IPPFA Retirement Guide (3rd Edition)

Windy City Publishers
www.windycitypublishers.com

Published in the United States of America

ISBN (3rd Edition):
978-1-953294-61-6

Library of Congress Control Number:
2021913428

Windy City Publishers
Chicago

To Illinois police and fire professionals:
active, retired and departed,
and their families

Illinois **P**ublic **P**ension **F**und **A**ssociation
An Association of Public Pension Funds
2587 Millennium Drive, Unit C
Elgin IL 60124, 630-784-0406
www.ippfa.org

CONTENTS

FOREWORD

Since 1985, the Illinois Public Pension Fund Association (IPPFA) has committed time and resources to assist local fire and police pension boards in administering benefits and investing funds to help public safety professionals achieve a secure retirement.

Along the way, we expanded our efforts to ensure that individual members had the ability to maximize their own retirement security and success. We have offered seminars and online material on benefits under the Illinois Pension Code as well as closely related municipal or other employer sponsored programs: Social Security, Section 457 Deferred Compensation, and retiree healthcare savings. Our IPPFA-TV site at YouTube brings much of this information directly to any user at any convenient time.

This book, first issued in 2021, is another tool in that ongoing effort. It brings together much of the information needed to understand and fully utilize benefits available to Illinois downstate and suburban police officers and firefighters. We trust that it will fulfill every reader's needs.

Importantly, this version includes a revised chapter on Social Security, incorporating the changes made late in 2024 in the *Social Security Fairness Act*. This law greatly impacted the Social Security benefits that most Illinois fire and police personnel will receive.

Please remember that beyond this information, there is no limit to the opportunity that you have to expand your personal knowledge of both the financial aspects of life after you stop working as well as the non-financial issues that you may face in retirement. Public sources (books, articles, websites, *etc.*) on these matters are virtually unlimited. And now, with the Social Security changes, much or most of what is written about that federal program will apply to our membership.

Don't let your pre-retirement and post-retirement education end with this book.

And most importantly, thank you for your commitment to the safety of our state.

~James McNamee
President
Illinois Public Pension Fund Association
January, 2025

INTRODUCTION

YOUR RETIREMENT INCOME IS DIFFERENT

Different in a lot of ways.

Like you, a neighbor who works at Motorola® and a brother who is a union plumber have pension plans that contribute to retirement security. But their pension plans are formed and governed under the federal Employee Retirement Income Security Act (ERISA). The US Department of Labor has regulatory oversight. The Pension Benefit Guarantee Corporation (PBGC) provides a base level of insurance should their private sector plans become insolvent. There are funding standards. The Board of Trustees has broad latitude to set benefits. It is unlikely that there is any payroll deduction to fund a portion of the benefit—the plan is fully paid for by the employer. There are strict rules protecting the pension rights of spouses, both those married to the pensioner and those who are divorced.

And the state has virtually no say in private sector benefits. Under the so-called ERISA "preemption," Illinois is prohibited by law from regulating private employee retirement benefits.

As for *your* pension, the environment and structure are very different. Illinois police or fire pensions are *not* governed by ERISA, or insured by any federal agency. State and local government pensions are effectively under the sole governance of the states. There is no insurance should a pension fund become insolvent. The Trustees in Illinois do not set benefits; the State of Illinois does. There is no pension "plan"—there is a pension law. And you, the employee, pay a substantial portion of your own pension via payroll deduction—a fact sometimes missed or understated.

As to other aspects of retirement income, your friends and relatives most likely participate in the Social Security system at work. You most likely do not, although some Illinois public safety workers do contribute. If you spend thirty years outside of Social Security, your federal benefits are greatly impacted.

Your personal savings rules are also different, at least those that govern tax-advantaged savings at work. Private corporate workers save through a 401(k) plan; charitable and educational groups through the 403(b). Your savings is under Section 457 of the Internal Revenue Code. Over the past decade, Section 457 rules have come very close to the 401(k) structure, but there are still differences. A news story or a public television show on workplace savings may not be fully applicable to you.

It is said that a secure retirement comes from a three-legged stool of retirement income—pension, Social Security, and personal savings. We'll look at each leg with emphasis on your unique situation as an Illinois public safety professional.

The first two chapters of this book discusses the Illinois pension systems that provide police and fire pension benefits under Articles 3 and 4 of the Illinois Pension Code.

A chapter follows on Social Security. The good news is that previously there were some specific provisions of federal law that reduced Social Security benefits for most Illinois fire and police professionals. Those were eliminated in 2024 under the *Social Security Fairness Act*. This updated version of our *IPPFA Retirement Guide* addresses those changes. This will help you better understand the Social Security benefits you might receive from work before your public safety career, part-time during your career, and for work after you leave the fire or police department.

Two chapters follow related to the "personal savings" leg of your retirement plan. Deferred Compensation under Section 457 is detailed in Chapter 4. And tax-advantaged savings specifically for retirement health care costs is covered in Chapter 5.

Public safety careers are no longer only filled by men. Efforts have been made to make the content of this book gender neutral. When the word "he" is used, it is done sparingly and only for the purpose of the conversational flow of the text. The purpose of this book is to explain your retirement benefits as they apply to you, non-Chicago municipal fire and police and fire district firefighters.

An Appendix reminds the reader of a valuable tax break for retired first responders related to their annual premium payments for medical and long-term care insurance.

This material is concise but thorough. It doesn't cover every law, rule or other element of retirement income, but it does hit on the areas that affect most police and firefighters outside of Chicago. Any questions remaining? Please contact us at IPPFA.

Illinois Public Pension Fund Association
Elgin, Illinois
January, 2025

DISCLAIMER

Public pensions, Social Security benefits, and deferred compensation arrangements are created and governed by laws. Such laws are subject to change and interpretation. The material in this book is presented solely for educational purposes to supplement and illuminate the information available to you from the only definitive sources: state and federal law. IPPFA, the contributors and the publisher are not offering legal or tax advice, or any other professional service. The reader should not make any decision that effects his or her retirement benefits without consultation with a pension or retirement board, the Social Security Administration, a deferred compensation company's credentialed agent, an attorney, a certified public accountant, or similarly qualified professional.

INFORMATION APPEARING ELSEWHERE

Some of the information presented appeared earlier in books by IPPFA project coordinator Dan Ryan. You may also see some of the material and even exact wording from Chapter 3 on the Downstate/Suburban Police Pension Funds appearing on pension fund or police department websites. This is because when Dan originally wrote some of this content in the form of the Skokie Police Pension Fund's *Guide to Retirement,* permission was given for any police department or pension fund to use the material. This permission remains in place, but any material duplicated was solely created by one of the authors, is the property of the author and is now licensed for use by IPPFA.

1 "DOWNSTATE" POLICE PENSIONS UNDER ARTICLE 3

OVERVIEW

Although called the "downstate" police pension system, the pension plan delineated in Article 3 of the Illinois Pension Code covers municipal police officers except for the largest city (whose officers are in a separate Chicago Police plan under Article 5) and the smallest cities under 5,000 in population (whose officers are in the Article 7 Illinois Municipal Retirement Fund). Note, however, that smaller communities may adopt an Article 3 police pension plan by referendum, and some have done so.

While police in Carbondale are actually downstate, so too are Waukegan and Galena, at least as far as their police pensions are concerned. For ease of communicating, IPPFA often refers to this group as the downstate and suburban police pension community.

This chapter explains the pension benefits payable to police retirees and survivors covered under the Article 3 systems. Benefits are no longer uniform: there is a different level of benefits for officers who were in Article 3 service prior to January 1st, 2011, and those first hired into Article 3 after that date. The "Tier 2" changes were made in every public pension plan in the state. Fortunately, upgrades were made in the downstate police and fire Tier 2 structure in January, 2020.

Where there is a difference in benefits, the chapter has separate sections. Where benefits are the same (*e.g.*, disability benefits, portability), no distinction between the Tiers is made.

SERVICE RETIREMENT BENEFITS—TIER 1

(IN ANY ARTICLE 3 SERVICE PRIOR TO JANUARY 1, 2011)

A Tier 1 officer is eligible for retirement benefits at age 50 if he or she has earned 20 years of creditable service, or retirement at age 60 if between 8 and 20 years have been earned.

TIER 1—Pension with 20 Years of Service

An officer age 50 or older with 20 years of creditable service is entitled to a pension equal to 50% of the salary attached to the rank on the police force at the time of retirement (or the average salary over the last year, if higher). For full years of service over 20 years, the officer will receive an additional 2.5% of salary for each year, to a maximum pension of 75% of salary. For example, an officer at age 50 or older, retiring after 26 years of service, will receive a pension of 65% of salary. If his annual salary was $90,000, the resulting pension of 65% would be $4,875 per month. At 30 years of service the 75% maximum pension would be $5,625 monthly.

A pension formula that is based on essentially your last day's rate of salary is very favorable to the retiring officer. But remember that this amount does not include overtime. You might retire at 75% of your base salary but this pension will not include any consideration of overtime. If you work a lot of overtime, you will not experience a replacement of 75% of your wages.

TIER 1—Pensions with Less than 20 Years of Service

An officer age 60 or older having at least 8, but less than 20 years of service, is entitled to a pension equal to 2.5% of salary for each year of service. An officer with at least 1 year, but less than 8 years of service, is also entitled to this benefit if he or she is receiving a retirement pension based on at least 8 years of service from another Illinois downstate police pension fund. Note that persons transferring departments after vesting in one pension fund may be affected by Public Act 100-0281. This law, in force as of 2019, governs pension eligibility under the fund into which a vested officer transfers. Guidance from the State on these transfers is still lacking and such a situation should be analyzed by all parties prior to making a transfer decision.

TIER 1—Increases in Pensions after Retirement

A pension increase occurs in the latter of the month after the retiree turns 55 or the month after he or she has been retired for one year. The increase is 3% for each year the officer has been receiving pension (or a prorated portion of 3% for partial years). For example, an officer retiring on his 52nd birthday would receive an increase of 9% the month after he turns 55 (calculated as 1/12 of 3% for the 36 month his pension has been paid). Then, on each subsequent January 1st, the officer will receive an additional increase of 3% of the pension then being received (*i.e.*, a compounded increase).

In another example, an officer who is already age 56 at the time of retirement will receive a 3% pension increase the first month after one year of retirement, and then another 3% each January 1st thereafter.

SERVICE RETIREMENT BENEFITS—TIER 2

(IN SERVICE AFTER JANUARY 1, 2011)

A Tier 2 officer is eligible for retirement benefits at age 55 upon attainment of 10 years of service. The pension is equal to 2.5% of his or her "final average salary" for each year of service. The "final average salary" is the average monthly salary during the last four years of service (technically, the highest 48 consecutive months within your last 60 months of service). Note that the law also allows the average salary calculation to consider the highest 96 consecutive months of salary within the last 120 months of service if that will produce a higher salary calculation. The highest allowable pension is 75% of final average salary.

For example, if an officer has 30 years of service and a four-year final average salary of $80,000 annually, the monthly pension would be $5,000.

If an officer with sufficient credit wishes to draw his or her pension prior to age 55, the pension may be started on or after age 50, but with a resulting decrease in the monthly amount. The decrease is 6% for each year the officer receives pension prior to age 55 (proportioned monthly). It is not clear at the date of publication if members are permitted to defer their pension beyond the date they are initially entitled to a reduced Tier 2 pension. IPPFA is working on this issue with the Department of Insurance.

NOTE

The Tier 2 law set the highest salary that can be used for calculation of the final average salary at $106,800.

This amount is then indexed for inflation in the future.

As of 2025, this cap had been indexed up to $141,407.

TIER 2—Increases in Pensions after Retirement

Upon reaching the latter of the January after the retiree turns age 60, or the January after he or she has been retired for one year, a retired Tier 2 officer will receive an increase in pension in the amount of one-half of the annual increase in the Consumer Price Index, but not more than 3%. Then, on each subsequent January 1st, the officer will receive an additional increase, calculated in the same manner, on the original amount of his or her pension. In other words, the annual increases in pension do not *compound*; they are simple increases on the original amount of pension.

ALL TIERS: RE-ENTRY AFTER RETIREMENT

An Article 3 retiree who returns to police work in the same department following a period on retirement pension will not be eligible for a higher pension amount unless he or she accrues a least five years of creditable service during the period of re-entered service.

DISABILITY PENSIONS

A pension will be paid to an officer, regardless of age, if the officer is physically or mentally disabled for service in the police department. Different levels of benefits are paid depending upon whether or not the medical condition is the result of a line-of-duty disability.

Line-of-Duty Disability Pensions

An officer who becomes disabled as a result of sickness, accident, or injury incurred in or resulting from the performance of an act of duty is entitled to either (a) a pension equal to 65% of salary or (b) the service retirement pension that the officer has earned by virtue of his or her years of service, whichever is higher. Examples: An officer with nine (9) years of service who is disabled in the line-of-duty would receive a pension of 65% of salary. An officer with 28 years of service similarly disabled would receive a pension of 70% of pay (the amount he would receive if he retired under normal circumstances). Note that the act of police duty that disabled an officer must involve a special risk in which an ordinary citizen would not participate.

These line-of-duty benefits are also payable if the disability is the result of certain occupational diseases for officers who work in combined police and fire departments.

Disability Pension—Not in Line of Duty

An officer who becomes disabled as a result of a cause other than performance of duty is entitled to a pension of 50% of salary.

Increases in Disability Pension—TIER 1

The monthly pension of an officer who retires on disability is increased January 1st of the year following his or her 60th birthday by 3% of the original pension for each completed year since the pension began. Subsequent increases of 3% of the original amount of pension occur on January 1st thereafter.

Increases in Disability Pension—TIER 2

The monthly pension of a Tier 2 officer who retires on disability is increased on January 1st following his or her 60th birthday by the lesser of 3% of the original benefit or one-half of the rate of inflation as established under the Pension Code. Subsequent increases using the same formula occur on each January 1st thereafter.

Qualifying for Disability Pension

An officer must be found to be disabled by the Board of Trustees upon examination by three (3) physicians selected by the Board, and the examination of other evidence of disability as determined to be necessary by the Trustees. The Board of Trustees will review the evidence of disability at a formal hearing, often with legal counsel to the Board present. An applicant also is entitled to have legal counsel present and may introduce any other relevant evidence of disability. Once retired on disability, the retiree must produce evidence of continuing disability each year, until attainment of age 50. *The burden of proving eligibility for a disability pension lies with the applicant.*

Benefits for Short-Term Disability

Benefits for disabling conditions which are not expected to result in permanent and total disability are payable under an employer's sick leave policy. Questions on these benefits should be referred to the Village or City Hall Personnel Office. However, female officers are entitled to non-duty disability pension benefits for pregnancy.

Converting a Police Disability to a Service Retirement Pension.

The Pension Code allows an officer who is retired on a disability pension to convert his or her status to a regular service retirement. This is not mandatory but is also not reversible once a conversion is made. To be eligible for such a conversion, the disability retiree must be at least 50 years old and have 20 or more years of pension participation when active time is added to the period of disability. If converted, the non-disability annual increases apply.

The salary that is considered when a disability pension is converted is the salary in effect at the time of the disability, unless the individual was hired prior to October 1, 1973. If the officer was hired before that date, then the pension is converted based on the salary in effect at the time of conversion.

If the officer had less than 20 years of active service, a disability pension is converted to a service pension in the amount of 50% of salary. If the officer had more than 20 years of active service, the officer coverts to a service retirement at the percentage of pay provided for in the Pension Code at the time he went on disability pension.

Note that survivors cannot convert a disability benefit; only the retired officer may so while still alive.

PENSIONS PAID TO SURVIVORS—TIER 1

(OFFICER IN ANY ARTICLE 3 SERVICE PRIOR TO JANUARY 1, 2011)

Pensions are usually payable to the surviving spouse of a retiree or active employee (but with special rules if the marriage occurred after retirement). For the surviving spouse of a retiree to be eligible, the parties must have been married at the time of retirement, or alternatively, the surviving spouse must qualify for a survivor's benefit under a new law Public Act 102-0811 which is effective on January 1, 2023. Under this change, a surviving spouse is eligible for a benefit if (i) the police officer was married to the surviving spouse for at least 5 years prior to the police officer's death and (ii) the surviving spouse has attained age 62. For a person who first becomes eligible for a benefit under this new subsection, the benefit shall begin to accrue on the effective date of this amendatory act of the 102nd General Assembly or the first day of the month following the police officer's death, whichever is later. Notwithstanding any other provision of the pension code, the benefits for a surviving spouse who qualifies under this change terminate no later than 15 years after the benefits begin to accrue.

It is unclear from this legislation whether or not the surviving spouse must be 62 or older at the date of the retiree's death or, if younger, may she or he receive benefits once age 62 is attained. It is also unclear if this new eligibility applies retroactively from the effective date of January 1, 2023. There may be other issues that arise from this new law that are not immediately identifiable at the time this book is being published. Police pension boards and their attorneys will be working to apply this change to circumstances that come up when police officers marry after retirement.

Gender is irrelevant under either a marriage or a civil union. Also, although benefits are described below as Surviving Spouse benefits, most survivor benefits may be payable to unwed natural or legally adopted children up to age 18, handicapped children regardless of age, or legally dependent parents when there is no surviving spouse. Note that there is no minimum age requirement for a survivor pension. Also, there is no requirement that a surviving spouse remain single in order to receive a police pension.

TIER 1—Spouse Surviving a Pension Recipient

When an officer who is receiving a pension dies, the surviving spouse is entitled to receive the pension that the officer was then receiving at the time of death.

Upon the death of a deferred pensioner (*i.e.,* a person who has worked long enough to vest for a benefit and has left the police department before retirement age), a pension is payable to the surviving spouse. The amount payable is the pension that would have been paid to a survivor had the retiree been age 50 (or 60 if applicable) and in receipt of his or her earned pension (*i.e.*, not deferred). However, the pension is not payable until the date upon which the deceased retiree, if living, would have reached the qualifying age for receipt of a pension (age 50 or age 60 for Tier 1 retirees). See *Thornley vs. River Forest Police Pension Fund.*

TIER 1—Spouse Surviving an Active Police Officer/ Death Not in the Line-of-Duty

Upon the death of an active officer who has earned at least 20 years of creditable service, the survivor will receive a pension equal to the amount that the officer had earned by virtue of his or her years of service. For example, the spouse of an officer who died after 22 years of service would receive a pension of 55% of salary.

Upon the death of an officer having at least 8, but less than 20 years of service, a survivor pension of 50% of salary is payable.

Upon the death of an officer having less than 8 years of service, no pension is payable. The estate of the officer is entitled to a refund of the officer's pension contributions to the Fund.

TIER 1—Spouse Surviving an Active Police Officer/ Line-of-Duty Death

Upon the death of an active officer who dies as a result of sickness, accident, or injury incurred in the performance of an act of duty, and who has not begun receiving either a retirement or disability pension, a surviving spouse is entitled to 100% of salary attached to the rank held by the deceased police officer on the last date of service. There is no service requirement to earn this benefit.

TIER 1—Increases in Survivor Pensions

The law does not provide for an annual increase to the pension received by a survivor of a Tier 1 officer. However, from time to time, the Illinois General Assembly and Governor may approve legislation to increase the minimum pension paid to survivors.

PENSIONS PAID TO SURVIVORS—TIER 2 (IN SERVICE AFTER JANUARY 1, 2011)

Pensions are often payable to the surviving spouse of a retiree or active employee. For a surviving spouse to be eligible, gender is irrelevant under either a marriage or civil union. **Please refer to the explanation of spouse eligibility that is discussed under Tier 1 survivor pensions on page 13**. Also, although benefits are described below as Surviving Spouse benefits, most survivor benefits may be payable to unwed natural or legally adopted children up to age 18, handicapped children regardless of age, or legally dependent parents when there is no surviving spouse. Note that there is no minimum age requirement for a survivor pension. Also, there is no requirement that a surviving spouse remain single in order to receive a pension.

TIER 2—Spouse Surviving a Pension Recipient

When an officer who is receiving a pension dies, the surviving spouse is entitled to receive survivor benefits in the amount of 66.67% of the pension the officer was receiving at the time of his or her death. Alternatively, a pension payable in the amount of 54% of the pensionable salary plus 12% per dependent child (to a maximum of 75% of pay) is paid if that amount is higher than 66.67% of the decedent's pension.

Upon the death of a deferred Tier 2 pensioner (*i.e.*, a person who has worked long enough to vest for a benefit and has left the police department before retirement age), a pension is payable to the surviving spouse. The age of the retiree or the survivor is irrelevant. The amount payable is the pension that would have been paid to a survivor had the retiree been age 55 and in receipt of his or her earned pension (*i.e.*, not deferred). However, the pension is not payable until the date upon which the deceased retiree, if living, would have reached the qualifying age for receipt of a pension (age 50 through 55 for Tier 2 retirees). See *Thornley vs. River Forest Police Pension Fund.*

TIER 2—Spouse Surviving an Active Police Officer/ Death Not in the Line-of-Duty

Upon the death of an active officer who has earned at least 10 years of creditable service, the surviving spouse is entitled to receive survivor benefits in the amount of 66.67% of the pension the officer was entitled to receive at the time of death (or the alternative payment of 54% of pensionable salary plus the dependent allowance referenced above.).

Upon the death of a Tier 2 officer having less than 10 years of service, no pension is payable. The estate of the officer is entitled to a refund of the officer's pension contributions to the Fund.

TIER 2—Spouse Surviving an Active Police Officer/ Line-of-Duty Death

Upon the death of an active officer who dies as a result of sickness, accident, or injury incurred in the performance of an act of duty, and who has not begun receiving either a retirement or disability pension, a surviving spouse is entitled to 100% of salary attached to the rank held by the deceased police officer on the last date of service. There is no service requirement to earn this benefit.

TIER 2—Increases in Survivor Pensions

The Tier 2 law provides for an increase in the pensions of survivors in a similar manner to the pensions for retired officers. The first increase occurs on the latter of the January after the spouse turns age 60, or the January after the spouse has been collecting benefits for one year.

EMPLOYEE CONTRIBUTIONS

Police pension benefits are partially funded by contributions made by active officers. Notably, public employees (particularly fire and police) pay for a meaningful portion of their own pension. Giving employees proper credit for the earnings on investment of their contributions from the first paycheck to the last pension check, public employees pay about 1/3 or more of their own pensions.

The Article 3 contribution rate is 9.91% of pensionable salary. Many cities and villages have adopted a so-called "employer pick-up" of contributions, a rule allowed under the Internal Revenue Code. This rule allows the contributions to be made on a tax-deferred basis, so the officer's taxable income goes down by 9.91%. When a pension is eventually paid, the pension is taxed and the IRS then gets its money.

An officer who does not earn a pension based on 20 years of service is entitled to a refund of contributions made. If the employee is rehired by the same police department and re-enters the pension fund, he or she must repay the contribution refund plus 2% annual interest in order to count the prior employment period as creditable service towards a pension benefit.

Refunds are eligible for a tax-deferred "rollover" to an Individual Retirement Account or other qualified pension plan that accepts such contributions. This allowance for a tax-deferred rollover was confirmed when the Illinois Public Pension Fund Association led a group of Illinois funds (yours probably included) to successfully petition the IRS for "qualified" status for Illinois Article 3 (police) and Article 4 (fire) pension funds.

TAXATION OF PENSION BENEFITS

Service pensions and pensions for survivors of service retirees are taxed under the federal tax law. Retirees may elect to have federal tax withheld from their pension checks. If your pension fund does not use "employer pick-up" or did not use it earlier in your career, a small portion of your pension will be exempt from federal taxation in accordance with IRS regulations at the time your pension is paid.

Taxation of pensions by state governments is governed by state law and Illinois does not currently tax pension payments. If you retire and move to another state that does tax pensions, it is probable that your Illinois pension fund *will not* provide for tax withholding for another state. You will have to make other arrangements for paying any non-Illinois state tax, such as making quarterly deposits.

Duty disability pensioners are not taxed at any level. The portion of a line-of-duty or occupational disease pension in excess of 65% of salary is subject to federal tax withholding and reporting, but most of these pension payments are not taxable. The non-taxability of the member's original duty-disability pension transfers to a survivor.

CREDITABLE SERVICE

Generally, creditable service is time served as a sworn officer in your community. Furloughs and suspensions of less than 30 days are counted, and leaves of absence of any length due to a personal accident, illness, or injury are counted. If a disabled officer returns to active service, up to 3 years of the period during which a disability pension was received are counted towards creditable service (if the officer makes the required contributions and works in active service for a period at least as long as the service being reinstated).

Under any circumstances, earning creditable service requires that the officer pay to the Fund the contributions that would have been paid had he or she been in actual police service.

Creditable service also includes service in the military forces of the United States entered into while an officer is on active police duty. Such military service is limited to five (5) years. There is also an opportunity for officers to purchase two years of credit for military service *prior* to entering police work. If this military service is to be counted as police pension creditable service, the officer needs to pay the employee contribution, interest, and an amount that represents the employer's cost. In other words, the officer pays the full cost of this military service.

Creditable service may also include time served as an officer in a police-related association.

PORTABILITY OF SERVICE FROM ANOTHER FUND

Transfer Between Illinois Article 3 Pension Funds

The pension laws allow creditable service in one Illinois Article 3 police pension fund to be transferred to another Article 3 fund under 40 ILCS5/3-110-d. This is called "portability." In explaining the opportunity to transfer credit from one Article 3 pension fund to another, we will use the phrase "current" to describe the department and pension fund to which the officer desires to transfer credit. Likewise, the "prior" department or fund is the pension plan covering the officer at his or her previous police department employer.

SPECIFICS: If an officer has at least two years of service in a prior department before transferring to the current department, the officer may arrange for that prior service to be transferred for credit into his or her current pension fund. The two-year requirement is waived if the officer left the prior fund due to a layoff or prior to the effective date of the act (August 17, 1997). The prior pension fund from which the officer is transferring will make a payment to the current pension fund in the amount of the officer's contributions made to the previous fund, 6% annual interest on those contributions (if a refund was taken, the money must be paid back to the prior fund with interest), plus a second amount that is also equal to the officer's contributions and interest (which is assumed to represent the municipality's share).

For example, after 2.5 years of service, a prior fund might transfer an officer's $20,000 in contributions, $1,000 in interest and an additional $21,000 for a total transfer to the current fund of $42,000.

However, if the current police pension fund finds that the amount transferred is less than the "true cost" (*i.e.* the full cost) of the creditable service being transferred, then either (a) the officer must pay the difference between the true cost and the amount being sent by the prior fund, or (b) the officer must accept the transfer of a reduced period of service, prorated based upon the portion of the true cost paid by the prior fund. Continuing the example from the paragraph above, if the current fund deems that 2.5 years of service has a true cost of $52,500, the officer could make up the $10,500 deficiency or accept transfer of a prorated 2.0 years of service.

Most pension funds allow an officer wishing to transfer credit to defer his or her decision until such time as a determination is made as to whether the officer will have to pay money to the current pension plan from his or her personal funds. Note that a calculation of the true cost must be performed by a qualified actuary retained by the current pension fund.

TRANSFER OF SERVICE TO ANOTHER FUND

In addition to within the Article 3 funds, Illinois law includes provisions for transfer of service from a police pension fund to certain other Illinois funds. Interested persons should check with those funds for any available options.

Those funds are:

- General Assembly Retirement System
- Illinois Municipal Retirement Fund
- State Employee's Retirement System
- Cook County Employee's Benefit Fund
- Sanitary District Employee's Benefit Fund

Transfer of Service between IMRF, SURS, and Chicago Police

At various times in the recent past there were opportunities to transfer service to Article 3 from IMRF, Illinois state university SURS and Chicago Police. Those opportunities have now closed but may again be authorized by the State Legislature at some point in the future.

GOVERNANCE

Legal Creation and Oversight

Illinois law governs your Article 3 pension fund. The Illinois Pension Code is Chapter 40 of the Illinois Compiled Statutes, 40 ILCS 5, and then the specific pension systems are created and regulated under separate articles. If you are a municipal officer outside of Chicago and not in the Illinois Municipal Retirement Fund, you are covered under Article 3 and also regulated by Article 1. Federal law plays only a small role in the areas of taxes on pensions and financial market disclosures.

Officers who review the pension statutes will note references to an option to participate in a self-managed plan instead of the defined benefit pension plan described in this book. However, such self-managed plans have not yet been established by the State of Illinois or any community.

The Board of Trustees

The Fund is governed by a Board of Trustees consisting of two officers elected by active officers, a retiree elected by retirees (including surviving spouses), and two citizens appointed by the mayor, or mayor and city council. The terms of the two active officer trustee positions run for two years and are usually staggered (one expires each year). Elections are held on the third Monday in April. The Trustees have a fiduciary responsibility to govern the Fund in a prudent manner within the requirements and limitations of Illinois law. Meetings are held quarterly and are open to the public except when personnel matters are discussed, as allowed by Illinois law. Trustees may not be paid for service as Trustees of the Fund.

Note that under Public Act 101-0610, responsibility for investment of your fund's assets was transferred to the Illinois Police Officers Pension Investment Fund. This is a nine-member trusteed fund whose board consists of active and retired police officers and municipal appointees with assistance from a professional administrator and consultants.

Role of the Illinois Department of Insurance

The Department of Insurance is authorized under the statutes to create rules governing pension administration, to regulate public pension funds, to audit public pension funds, and to report to the Legislature as to the valuation of these funds. The Public Pension Section handles these responsibilities. The department is an active participant in protecting public employee pensions. They may be contacted at the Public Pension Section, Illinois Department of Insurance, 320 W. Washington St., Springfield, IL 62767.

Member Data for Participation

To ensure coverage and benefits under the Pension Fund, officers should apply for participation and complete the pension fund's necessary forms. Note that the Illinois Department of Insurance requires that information on marital status, children, and your birth certificate be kept in the pension fund's records. If your information is always up to date, this will help ensure timely processing of your benefits, especially if a catastrophic event occurs. Also, since it is a requirement of the pension fund that this data be maintained, keeping your records current will help your pension fund stay in compliance with the Department of Insurance rules.

Administrative Review

Final administrative decisions of the Board of Trustees are subject to judicial review under the Illinois Administrative Review Law.

Role of the City or Village Government

The municipal treasurer is responsible for the collecting of funds, disbursing of pensions, and custodianship of invested funds until the transfer to the consolidated police investment fund. The mayor and board or council levy local taxes to support police pensions. Although the Article 3 Police Pension Fund is an autonomous entity, the Pension Board of Trustees may adopt specifically or by practice the municipality's policies regarding accounting records, budgetary practices, training reimbursement, and expense reimbursement.

Pension matters can get quite complicated. The pension fund, the police department, and the municipal government should attempt to coordinate any pension related matters when possible to serve the best interest of active and retired officers pursuant to Illinois law. As an example, the status of an injured officer may involve the department (*e.g.*, rules regarding light duty), the municipality (*e.g.*, their handling of a related worker compensation case), and the pension fund (*e.g.*, processing of an application for a line-of-duty disability pension).

It is difficult to promulgate hard and fast policies to govern such situations. Coordination and cooperation by all parties, if possible, can add great value.

Role of Professional Consultants

To assist the pension Board of Trustees in carrying out their duties, the Fund may retain a qualified actuary, certified public accountant, banks, and independent legal counsel. Since the Illinois Department of Insurance provides an actuarial valuation, and the municipality will retain a CPA for a comprehensive audit, a pension plan may decide not to hire its own experts in those areas.

As the funds have grown in number of participants and the laws have become more complex (pension portability, public meeting compliance, *etc.*), some Article 3 police funds have retained companies to provide pension fund administrative services. Besides current financial reporting and expertise on the pension rules, the service provided to the trust *and the membership* may be better than a group of volunteer board members can deliver on their own.

Role of Illinois Police Officer Pension Investment Fund

Beginning in 2022, investment of police pension fund assets became the responsibility of the IPOPIF. This investment fund is governed by a Board consisting of active and retired police offices and municipal officials. Your local pension fund keeps funds on hand to pay benefits and can draw from the IPOPIF as needed to cover pension and administrative costs.

ANYTHING ELSE YOU SHOULD DO?

You may wish to go to the statute for more detailed information. Put "Illinois Pension Code" in a Google search and then pick Article 3 from the listings that result.

Attending a board meeting of your Article 3 fund is always a good idea, along with voting on the active or retired trustee positions.

Some of the larger pension systems in the state assist the retiree with retiree health insurance. Very few of the Article 3 (police) and Article 4 (fire) systems provide any relief for the high cost of retiree health insurance. You need to become an expert in this expense as retirement approaches.

Remember that your pension does not include any replacement of your overtime wages.

2 "DOWNSTATE" FIRE PENSIONS UNDER ARTICLE 4

OVERVIEW

Although called the "downstate" fire pension system, the pension plan delineated in Article 4 of the Illinois Pension Code covers fire district and municipal firefighters except for the largest city (whose firefighters are in a separate Chicago Fire plan under Article 6) and the smallest cities under 5,000 in population (whose firefighters are in the Article 7 Illinois Municipal Retirement Fund). Note, however, that smaller communities may adopt an Article 4 fire pension plan by referendum.

While firefighters in Decatur are actually downstate, so too are Deerfield-Bannockburn and Rockford, at least as their fire pensions are concerned.

This chapter explains the pension benefits payable to fire retirees and survivors covered under the Article 4 systems. Benefits are no longer uniform: there is a different level of benefits for firefighters who were in Article 4 service prior to January 1st, 2011, and those first hired into Article 4 after that date. The "Tier 2" changes were made in every public pension plan in the state. Fortunately, improvements were made in the downstate police and fire Tier 2 structure in January, 2020.

Where there is a difference in benefits, the chapter has separate sections. Where benefits are the same (*e.g.*, disability benefits, reciprocity), no distinction between the Tiers is made.

SERVICE RETIREMENT BENEFITS—TIER 1

(IN ANY ARTICLE 4 SERVICE PRIOR TO JANUARY 1, 2011)

A Tier 1 firefighter is eligible for benefits at retirement at age 50 if he or she has earned 20 years of creditable service or retirement at age 60 if between 10 and 20 years have been earned.

TIER 1—Pension with 20 Years of Service

A firefighter age 50 or older with 20 years of creditable service is entitled to a pension equal to 50% of the salary attached to the rank on the fire department at the time of retirement. For years of service over 20 years, the firefighter will receive an additional 2.5% of salary for each year, to a maximum pension of 75% of salary. For example, a firefighter retiring after 26 years would receive a pension at age 50 or older of 65% of salary. Note that the formula also recognizes partial years of service, so a firefighter who worked 28-1/2 years would receive a pension of 71.25% of salary. This latter employee, if his salary was $90,000, would receive a monthly pension of $5,344.

TIER 1—Pensions with Less than 20 Years of Service

A firefighter age 60 or older having at least 10, but less than 20 years of service, is entitled to a pension detailed in Section 4-109(b) as follows:

10 Years of Service	15.0% of salary
11 Years of Service	17.6% of salary
12 Years of Service	20.4% of salary
13 Years of Service	23.4% of salary
14 Years of Service	26.6% of salary
15 Years of Service	30.0% of salary
16 Years of Service	33.6% of salary
17 Years of Service	37.4% of salary
18 Years of Service	41.4% of salary
19 Years of Service	45.6% of salary

TIER 1—Increases in Pensions after Retirement

A pension increase occurs in the latter of the month after the retiree turns 55 or the month after he or she has been retired for one year. The increase is 3% for each year the retiree has been receiving pension (or a prorated portion of 3% for partial years). For example, a firefighter retiring on his 52nd birthday would receive an increase of 9% the month after he turns 55 (calculated as 1/12 of 3% for the 36 month his pension has been paid). Then, on each subsequent January 1st, the retiree will receive an additional increase of 3% of the pension then being received (*i.e.*, a compounded increase).

In another example, a firefighter who is already age 56 at the time of retirement will receive a 3% pension increase the first month after one year of retirement, and then another 3% each January 1st thereafter.

SERVICE RETIREMENT BENEFITS—TIER 2

(IN SERVICE AFTER JANUARY 1, 2011)

A Tier 2 firefighter is eligible for retirement benefits at age 55 upon attainment of 10 years of service. The pension is equal to 2.5% of his or her "final average salary" for each year of service. The "final average salary" is the average monthly salary during the last four years of service (technically, the highest 48 consecutive months within your last 60 months of service). Note that the law also allows the average salary calculation to consider the highest 96 consecutive months of salary within the last 120 months of service if that will produce a higher salary calculation. The highest allowable pension is 75% of final average salary.

So, for example, if a firefighter has 30 years of service and an four-year final average salary of $80,000 annually, the monthly pension would be $5,000.

If a firefighter with sufficient credit wishes to draw his or her pension prior to age 55, the pension may be started on or after age 50, but with a resulting decrease in the monthly amount. The decrease is 6% annually for each year that the firefighter receives pension prior to age 55 (proportioned monthly). It is not clear at the date of publication if members are permitted to defer their pension beyond the date they are initially entitled to a reduced Tier 2 pension. IPPFA is working on this issue with the Department of Insurance.

NOTE

The Tier 2 law set the highest salary that can be used for calculation of the final average salary at $106,800.

This amount is then indexed for inflation in the future.

As of 2025, this cap had been indexed up to $141,407.

TIER 2—Increases in Pensions after Retirement

Upon reaching the latter of January after the retiree turns age 60 or January after he or she has been retired for one year, a retired Tier 2 firefighter will receive an increase in pension in the amount of one-half of the annual increase in the Consumer Price Index, but not more than 3%. Then, on each subsequent January 1st, the firefighter will receive an additional increase, calculated in the same manner, on the original amount of his or her pension. In other words, the annual increases in pension do not "compound;" they are simple increases on the original amount of pension.

ALL TIERS: RE-ENTRY AFTER RETIREMENT

An Article 4 fire retiree who returns to sworn fire service in the same department following a period on retirement pension will not be eligible for a higher pension amount unless he or she accrues a least three years of creditable service during the period of re-entered service.

DISABILITY PENSIONS

A pension will be paid to a firefighter, regardless of age, if the firefighter is physically or mentally disabled for service in the fire department. Different levels of benefits are paid depending upon whether or not the medical condition is the result of a line-of-duty disability. There is no age requirement for a disability pension.

Line-of-Duty Disability Pensions

A firefighter who becomes disabled as a result of sickness, accident, or injury incurred in or resulting from the performance of an act of duty is entitled to either (a) a pension equal to 65% of salary or (b) the service retirement pension that the firefighter has earned by virtue of his or her years of service, whichever is higher. Examples: A firefighter with 10 years of service who is disabled in the line-of-duty would receive a pension of 65% of salary. A firefighter with 28 years of service similarly disabled would receive a pension of 70% of pay (the amount he or she would receive if retired under normal circumstances). An additional payment is made in the amount of $20 per month for each unwed child under age 18 or each disabled child, as long as the total payment to the disabled firefighter does not exceed 75% of salary.

Occupational Disease Disability Pension

For firefighters who have completed five years of creditable service, Article 4 pension benefits for line-of-duty disability are expanded under Section 4-110.1 of the code to include disabilities that result from heart disease, stroke, tuberculosis, any disease of the lung or respiratory tract, and cancers caused by exposure to heat, radiation, or a known carcinogen as defined by the International Agency for Research on Cancer.

Disability Pension—Not in Line of Duty

A firefighter with seven years of service who becomes disabled as a result of a cause other than performance of fire duty is entitled to a pension of 50% of salary. Note that a recent court decision clarified that the seven years of service needed to qualify for a non-duty disability pension must be served with the member's current department. Reciprocal service in prior pension fund does not count towards the seven years.

Increases in Disability Pension—TIER 1

The monthly pension of a firefighter who retires on disability pension is increased each January 1st of the year following his or her 60th birthday, by 3% of the original pension for each completed year since the pension began. If a firefighter is receiving an additional dependent benefit for a line-of-duty or occupational disease disability, the dependent payment is increased 3%, compounded every January following the start of the dependent benefit, regardless of the age of the firefighter.

Increases in Disability Pension—TIER 2

The monthly pension of a Tier 2 officer who retires on disability is increased on January 1st following his or her 60th birthday by the lesser of 3% of the original benefit or one-half of the rate of inflation as established under the Pension Code. Subsequent increases using the same formula occur on each January 1st thereafter.

Qualifying for Disability Pension

A firefighter must be found to be disabled by the Board of Trustees upon examination by three (3) physicians selected by the Board and the examination of other evidence of disability as determined to be necessary by the Trustees. The Board of Trustees will review the evidence of disability at a formal hearing, often with legal counsel to the Board present. An applicant is entitled to have legal counsel present also and may introduce any other relevant evidence of disability. Once retired on disability, the retiree must produce evidence of continuing disability each year, until attainment of age 50. *The burden of proving eligibility for a disability pension lies with the applicant.*

Benefits for Short-Term Disability

Benefits for disabling conditions which are not expected to result in permanent and total disability are payable under an employer's sick leave policy. Questions on these benefits should be referred to the Village or City Hall or Fire Protection District Personnel Office.

Converting a Fire Disability to a Service Retirement Pension.

The Pension Code allows a firefighter who is retired on a disability pension to convert his or her status to a regular service retirement. This is not mandatory but is also not reversible once a conversion is made. To be eligible for such a conversion, the disability retiree must be at least 50 years old and have 20 or more years of pension participation when active time is added to the period of disability. If converted, the non-disability annual increases apply.

If the firefighter had less than 20 years of active service, a disability pension is converted to a service pension in the amount of 50% of salary. The salary used for this calculation is the salary used to compute the disability pension when the firefighter first retired. Note that the initial conversion benefit cannot be less than the original disability benefit.

If the firefighter had 20 or more years of active service, the retiree coverts to a service retirement at the percentage of pay provided for in the Pension Code at the time he went on disability pension. Further, the salary used for the calculation is the salary in effect at the time of conversion from disability to service retiree status.

Note that survivors cannot convert a disability benefit; only the retired officer may so while still alive.

PENSIONS PAID TO SURVIVORS—TIER 1

(FIREFIGHTER IN ANY ARTICLE 4 SERVICE PRIOR TO JANUARY 1, 2011)

Pensions may be payable to the surviving spouse of a retiree (married to the retiree at the time of retirement or married for at least one year) or active employee. Although benefits are described below as Surviving Spouse benefits, survivor benefits may be payable to natural or legally adopted (and unwed) children up to age 18, handicapped children regardless of age, or legally dependent parents when there is no surviving spouse. For a surviving spouse to be eligible, gender is irrelevant under either a marriage or a civil union. Note that there is no minimum age requirement for a survivor pension. Also, there is no continuing requirement that a surviving spouse remain single in order to receive a pension.

TIER 1—Spouse Surviving a Pension Recipient

When a firefighter who is receiving a pension dies, the surviving spouse is entitled to receive a benefit equal to the greater of 100% of the monthly pension that the retiree was receiving at the time death *or* 54% of the pensionable salary used to calculate the pension (plus an additional 12% for any qualifying dependent child to a maximum of 75% of pay).

Upon the death of a deferred pensioner (*i.e.*, a person who has worked long enough to vest for a benefit and has left the fire department before retirement age), a pension is payable to an eligible surviving spouse. The age of the retiree or the survivor is irrelevant. The amount payable is the pension that would have been paid to a survivor had the retiree been age 50 and in receipt of his or her earned pension (*i.e.*, not deferred). However, note that in a police pension lawsuit judgment, it was determined that the pension is not payable until the date upon which the deceased retiree, if living, would have reached the qualifying age for receipt of a pension (age 50 or age 60 for Tier 1 retirees). This may or may not be found to apply to fire pensions. See *Thornley vs. River Forest Police Pension Fund.*

TIER 1—Spouse Surviving an Active Firefighter/ Death Not in the Line-of-Duty

Upon the death of an active firefighter who dies not as a result of a line-of-duty event, the surviving spouse is entitled to receive the benefit the fire-fighter is entitled to by virtue of his or her service (or a higher amount based on 54% of pensionable salary plus 12% for qualifying dependents to a maximum of 75% of salary).

TIER 1—Spouse Surviving an Active Firefighter/ Line-of-Duty Death

Upon the death of an active firefighter who dies as a result of sickness, accident, or injury incurred and resulting from the performance of an act of duty, who without having begun to receive either a retirement pension or disability pension, is entitled to 100% of salary attached to the rank held by the deceased firefighter on the last date of service.

TIER 1—Increases in Survivor Pensions

The law does not provide for an annual increase to the pension received by a survivor of a Tier 1 firefighter. However, from time to time, the Illinois General Assembly and Governor may approve legislation to increase the minimum pension paid to survivors.

PENSIONS PAID TO SURVIVORS—TIER 2

(IN SERVICE AFTER JANUARY 1, 2011)

Pensions may be payable to the surviving spouse of a Tier 2 retiree (married to the retiree at the time of retirement or married for at least one year) or active employee. Although benefits are described below as Surviving Spouse benefits, survivor benefits may be payable to natural or legally adopted (and unwed) children up to age 18, handicapped children regardless of age, or legally dependent parents when there is no surviving spouse. Note that there is no minimum age requirement for a survivor pension. For a surviving spouse to be eligible, gender is irrelevant under either a marriage or a civil union. Also, there is no continuing requirement that a surviving spouse remain single in order to receive a pension.

TIER 2—Spouse Surviving a Pension Recipient

When a firefighter who is receiving a pension dies, the surviving spouse is entitled to receive survivor benefits in the amount of 66.67% of the pension the firefighter was receiving at the time of his or her death. Alternatively, payment of 54% of salary upon which the pension was based plus 12% for any qualifying dependent child may be paid if that will result in a higher monthly pension (to a 75% maximum).

Upon the death of a deferred Tier 2 fire pensioner (*i.e.*, a person who has worked long enough to vest for a benefit and has left the fire department before retirement age), a pension is payable to an eligible surviving spouse. The age of the retiree or the survivor is irrelevant. The amount payable is the pension that would have been paid to a survivor had the retiree been age 55 and in receipt of his or her earned pension (*i.e.*, not deferred). However, note that in a police pension lawsuit judgment, it was determined that the pension is not payable until the date upon which the deceased retiree, if living, would have reached the qualifying age for receipt of a pension (age 50 through 55 for Tier 2 retirees). This may or may not be found to apply to fire pensions. See *Thornley vs. River Forest Police Pension Fund.*

TIER 2—Spouse Surviving an Active Firefighter/ Death Not in the Line-of-Duty

Upon the death of an active firefighter from a non-line-of-duty event, the surviving spouse is entitled to receive survivor benefits in the amount of 66.67% of the pension the firefighter was entitled to receive at the time of death (or the alternative payment of 54% of pensionable salary plus dependent allowance referenced above.).

TIER 2—Spouse Surviving an Active Firefighter/ Line-of-Duty Death

Upon the death of an active firefighter who dies as a result of sickness, accident, or injury incurred in the performance of an act of duty, and who has not begun receiving either a retirement or disability pension, a surviving spouse is entitled to 100% of salary attached to the rank held by the deceased firefighter on the last date of service.

TIER 2—Increases in Survivor Pensions

The Tier 2 law provides for an increase in the pensions of survivors in a similar manner to the pensions for retired firefighters. The first increase occurs on the latter of January after the spouse turns age 60 or January after the spouse has been collecting benefits for one year.

EMPLOYEE CONTRIBUTIONS

The pension benefits are partially funded by contributions made by active firefighters. Notably, public employees pay for a meaningful portion of their own pension, particularly fire and police. If public employees are given proper credit for the investment earnings on their contributions, from the first paycheck to the last pension check, it is estimated that these workers pay for 1/3 or more of their own pension.

The Article 4 contribution rate is 9.455% of pensionable salary (excluding overtime). Many cities, villages and fire districts have adopted a so-called “employer pick-up” of contributions, a rule allowed under the Internal Revenue

Code. This rule allows the contributions to be made on a tax-deferred basis, so the firefighter's taxable income goes down 9.455%. When a pension is eventually paid, the pension is taxed and the IRS then gets its money.

A firefighter who does not earn a pension based on 20 years of service is entitled to a refund of contributions made. If the employee is rehired by the same fire department and re-enters the pension fund, he or she must repay the contribution refund plus 2% annual interest in order to count the prior employment as creditable service towards a fire pension benefit.

Refunds are eligible for a tax-deferred "rollover" to an Individual Retirement Account or other qualified pension plan that accepts such contributions. This allowance for a tax-deferred rollover was confirmed when the Illinois Public Pension Fund Association led a group of Illinois funds (yours probably included) to successfully petition the IRS for "qualified" status for Illinois Article 3 (police) and Article 4 (fire) pension funds.

TAXATION OF PENSION BENEFITS

Payments to service retirees and survivors of service pensioners are taxed under the federal tax law. If your pension fund does not use "employer pick-up" or did not use it earlier in your career, a small portion of your pension will be exempt from federal taxation in accordance with IRS regulations at the time your pension is paid. Retirees may elect to have federal tax withheld from their pension checks.

Taxation of pensions by state governments is governed by state law and Illinois does not currently tax pension payments. If you retire in another state that does tax pensions, it is probable that your Illinois pension fund will not provide for tax withholding for another state. You will have to make other arrangements to pay non-Illinois state tax, such as making quarterly payments.

Line-of-duty disability and occupational disease pensions are not taxed at the federal level, nor are benefits paid to survivors of such pensioners. The portion of a line-of-duty or occupational disease pension in excess of 65% of salary is subject to federal tax withholding and reporting, but most of these pension payments are not taxable.

CREDITABLE SERVICE

Generally, creditable service is time served as a firefighter in your community. Furloughs and suspensions of less than 30 days are counted and leaves of absence of any length due to a personal accident, illness, or injury are counted. If a disabled firefighter returns to active service, up to 3 years of the period during which a disability pension was received are counted towards creditable service (if the firefighter makes the required contributions and works in active service for a period at least as long as the service being reinstated).

Under any circumstances, earning of creditable service requires that the firefighter pay to the Fund the contributions that would have been paid had he or she been in actual fire service.

Creditable service also includes service in the military forces of the United States entered into while a firefighter is on active fire duty. Such military service is limited to 5 years. There is also an opportunity for firefighters to purchase two years of credit for military service prior to entering the fire service. If this military service is to be counted as fire pension creditable service, the firefighter needs to pay the employee contribution, interest, and an amount that represents the employer's cost. In other words, the firefighter pays the whole cost of obtaining credit for this military service.

There are numerous provisions of Article 4 that award credited service or allow transfer of service to the benefit of one person or a small group of people. For example, credited service is awarded for duty as a fire inspector between 1976 and 1988 if the service was in a municipality of under 10,000 in population located in a county with a population over 3 million. Another example: until 1989 an active member of the Illinois Municipal Retirement Fund who is a county sheriff could transfer service from an Article 4 fire fund to the IMRF.

These examples are most likely not important to anyone reading this book other than showcasing the type of provisions that can be included in Illinois pension statutes.

RECIPROCITY AMONG ARTICLE 4 FIRE PENSION FUNDS

The state law includes a provision allowing "reciprocity" between Article 4 pension funds. This is different than the Article 3 police funds allowance for "portability." Using **portability**, a police officer moves his or her service and money from one police pension fund to another. Under fire fund ***reciprocity***, the firefighter leaves his or her service (and money) in each pension fund in which they participated and ultimately receives a pension from multiple funds.

In the Article 4 fire fund reciprocity arrangement, the pension code provides for the opportunity for a member to receive a pension from a community where he or she worked for a period of time short of the time required for **vesting** as long as the employee accumulates enough time in total in Article 4 funds to qualify for a pension.

The best way to explain reciprocity is to use an example.

> Robert was a firefighter in LeClaire, IL for four years and then moves to the department in Ashton, IL for eighteen years. He has a total of twenty-two years of Article 4 fire fund service when he retires.
>
> To maintain his service at LeClaire Fire, Robert either leaves his contributions in the LeClaire Fire Pension Fund or pays back any refund he took. Either way, if he wants to reciprocate his service between the funds, he owes LeClaire an additional 1% of pay in contributions plus 6% annual interest as well as 6% annual interest on any refund he took out.
>
> Over at Ashton, his payroll contribution goes up 1% of pay for all Ashton pensionable salary if he wishes to combine Ashton service with another fire fund.
>
> Robert elects reciprocity and at retirement he receives:
>
> A pension from the LeClaire Fire Pension Fund for his four years of service there, which will be 10% of the salary attached to his rank when he left LeClaire. The 10% figure is based on 1/12 of 2.5% of

his final salary for each month of service completed in LeClaire (which is the standard Article 4 formula).

A pension from the Ashton Fire Pension Fund calculated as follows: 55% of the salary attached to the rank when he left Ashton (55% is based on the total of twenty-two years at LeClaire *and* Ashton combined times 2.5%) *minus* the amount Robert is paid by the LeClaire Fire Pension Fund.

A dollar example using the hypothetical service above follows based on Robert's salary as a firefighter being $3,500 a month when he left LeClaire and his salary when he left Ashton eighteen years later as a lieutenant being $7,000 a month.

PENSION FROM LECLAIRE:

48 months x 1/12 x 2.5% (10%) times his monthly salary of $3,500	$ 350

PENSION FROM ASHTON:

Twenty-two years x 2.5% (55%) times his monthly salary of $7,000, minus the $350 paid by the LeClaire Fire Pension	$3,500
Total Pension	**$3,850**

The Ashton Fire Pension Fund gets a little beat up in this process. They are paying Robert a pension based on $7,000 in monthly salary including his four years at LeClaire which is costing Ashton $700 a month. For that they only get to drop their total payment by the $350 that LeClaire is paying. But Ashton *did* get a little higher payroll contribution from Robert (1% of salary), so that might compensate them. But if Robert retires at a higher rank or possibly as the Chief of Department at Ashton, the Ashton Fire Pension Fund may take a pretty good hit on reciprocity. LeClaire is only going to pay $350 a month of Robert's pension no matter what his final career salary.

If an active firefighter becomes entitled to a disability pension after all reciprocity costs have been paid, payment of disability benefits is handled as follows. First, a duty or non-duty disability is paid by the current fund. However, for an occupational disease benefit, a portion of the benefit is paid by each reciprocal fund, prorated based on the firefighter's service with each fund.

There are notice requirements related to reciprocity for any person first hired into Article 4 service after July 1, 2004. To obtain reciprocal credit, a person must notify his current employer, his previous Article 4 employers *and* the Illinois Department of Insurance (Public Pension Fund Section) of his or her intent to receive reciprocal benefits. *Such notification must be made within twenty-one months of being hired.* For Tier 2 members, notification can be delayed to the latter of twenty-one months of being hired by the current fund or April 9, 2023.

There are some other reciprocity rules that are not easily reflected in the example noted above. First, Article 4 participants must have at least one year of service in any fire department for which they wish to claim reciprocal service. Also, a person must have at least three years of service in his or her final fire department in order to make reciprocity work. Repayment of a refund to a fire pension fund may be made in installments for up to ten years, but must be fully paid prior to retirement.

TRANSFER OF SERVICE TO ANOTHER FUND

Illinois law also includes provisions for transfer of service from a fire pension fund to certain other Illinois funds. Interested parties should check with these systems regarding transfer options.

Those funds are:

- General Assembly Retirement System
- Illinois Municipal Retirement Fund
- State Employee's Retirement System
- Cook County Employee's Benefit Fund
- Sanitary District Employee's Benefit Fund

GOVERNANCE

Legal Creation and Oversight

Illinois law governs your Article 4 pension fund. The Illinois Pension Code is Chapter 40 of the Illinois Compiled Statutes, 40 ILCS 5, and then the specific pension systems are created and regulated under separate articles. If you are a municipal firefighter outside of Chicago and not in the Illinois Municipal Retirement Fund, you are covered under Article 4 and also regulated by Article 1. Federal law plays only a small role in taxing pensions and financial market disclosure.

Firefighters who review the pension statutes will note references to an option to participate in a self-managed plan instead of the defined benefit pension plan described in this book. However, such self-managed plans have not yet been established by the State of Illinois or any community.

The Board of Trustees

The Fund is governed by a Board of Trustees consisting of two firefighters elected by active firefighters, a retiree elected by retirees, and two citizens appointed by the mayor or mayor and city council (or similar officers in a fire protection district). The terms of the two active firefighter trustee positions run for three years and are usually staggered. Elections are held on the third Monday in April. The Trustees have a fiduciary responsibility to govern the Fund in a prudent manner within the requirements and limitations of Illinois law. Meetings are held quarterly and are open to the public except when personnel matters are discussed, as allowed by Illinois law. Trustees may not be paid for service as Trustees of the Fund.

Note that under Public Act 101-0610, responsibility for investment of your fund's assets will be transferred by June, 2022 to the Illinois Firefighters Pension Investment Fund. This is a nine-member trusteed fund whose board consists of active and retired firefighters and municipal appointees with assistance from a professional administrator and consultants.

Role of the Illinois Department of Insurance

The Department of Insurance is authorized under the statutes to create rules governing pension administration, to regulate public pension funds, to audit public pension funds, and to report to the Legislature as to the valuation of these funds. The Public Pension Section handles these responsibilities. The entire department and the pension section are active participants in protecting public employee pensions. They may be contacted at the Public Pension Section, Illinois Department of Insurance, 320 W. Washington St., Springfield, IL 62767.

Member Data for Participation

To ensure coverage and benefits under the Pension Fund, firefighters should apply for participation and complete the pension fund's necessary forms. Note that the Illinois Department of Insurance requires that information on marital status, children, and your birth certificate be kept in the pension fund's records. If your information is always up to date, this will help ensure timely processing of your benefits, especially if a catastrophic event occurs. Also, since it is a requirement for this data to be maintained, keeping your records current will help your pension fund stay in compliance with the Department of Insurance rules.

Administrative Review

Final administrative decisions of the Board of Trustees are subject to judicial review under the Illinois Administrative Review Law.

Role of the City or Village Government

The municipal or district treasurer is the Treasurer of the Fire Pension Fund by law and is responsible for the collecting of funds, disbursing of pensions, and custodianship of invested funds (until 2021/2022). The mayor and board or council (or fire district board) levy local taxes to support fire pensions. Although the Article 4 Fire Pension Fund is an autonomous entity, the Pension Board of Trustees may adopt specifically or by practice the municipality's policies regarding accounting records, budgetary practices, training reimbursement, and expense reimbursement.

Pension matters can get quite complicated. The pension fund, the fire department, and the municipal or district government should attempt to coordinate any pension related matters when possible to serve the best interest of active and retired firefighters pursuant to Illinois law. As an example, the status of an injured firefighter may involve the department (*e.g.*, rules regarding light duty), the municipality (*e.g.*, their handling of a related worker compensation case), and the pension fund (*e.g.*, processing of an application for a line-of-duty disability pension).

Not everything can be foreseen and written into hard and fast policies. Coordination and cooperation by all parties, if possible, can add great value.

Role of Professional Consultants

To assist the Board of Trustees in carrying out their duties, the Fund may retain a qualified actuary, certified public accountant, bankers, and independent legal counsel. Since the Illinois Department of Insurance provides an actuarial valuation and the municipality or fire district will retain a CPA for a comprehensive audit, a pension plan may decide not to hire its own experts in those areas.

As the funds have grown in number of participants and the laws have become more complex (pension reciprocity, public meeting compliance, *etc.*), some Article 4 fire funds have retained companies to provide pension fund administrative services. Besides current financial reporting and expertise on the pension rules, the service provided to the trust *and the membership* may be better than a group of volunteer trustees can deliver on their own.

Role of Firefighters Pension Investment Fund

Beginning in 2021/2022, investment of police pension fund assets became the responsibility of the FPIF. This investment fund is governed by a Board consisting of active and retired firefighters and municipal officials. Your local pension fund keeps funds on hand to pay benefits and can draw from the FPIF as needed to cover pension and administrative costs.

ANYTHING ELSE YOU SHOULD DO?

You may wish to go to the statute for more detailed information. Put "Illinois Pension Code" in a Google search and then pick Article 4 from the listings that result.

Pension plans that retain professional firms for fund administration may have access to that company's training programs on Article 4 pension benefits.

Attending a board meeting of your Article 4 fund is always a good idea, along with voting on the active or retired trustee positions.

Some of the larger pension systems in the state assist the retiree with retiree health insurance. Very few of the Article 3 (police) and Article 4 (fire) systems provide any relief for the high cost of retiree health insurance. You need to become an expert in this expense as retirement approaches.

3 SOCIAL SECURITY

There are two types of fire and police professionals reading this chapter: those who are enrolled in Social Security during their public safety careers and those who are not. *Most of you in Illinois are not in Social Security.* For those of you who are in Social Security at the firehouse or police station, Social Security will be a full, strong leg in your retirement income. For those working outside of Social Security, the thirty or so years you spend in work outside of Social Security reduces those benefits when compared to what your private-sector friends and relatives will receive.

Up until right now, 2025, there were provisions of the Social Security Act that reduced benefits for retirees who had pensions from work outside of Social Security. These two provisions, the Windfall Elimination Provision (WEP) and the Government Pension Offset (GPO) were repealed in early 2025 by an act of Congress and signature by the President. The law, the *Social Security Fairness Act*, is retroactive to December 2023. So as you read this book, whether you are in Social Security or excluded as a first-responder, the same Social Security laws and formulas apply to you.

In previous editions of this book and in other training material, IPPFA provided a detailed explanation of the WEP and the GPO. This is no longer necessary and they are not addressed in this book, other than to emphasize their repeal. Instead, we now provide a basic overview of Social Security and instructions on where to go for more detailed information.

During the discussion, this chapter alternatively uses the familiar "SSA" for Social Security, as in Social Security Act or Social Security Administration.

WHAT'S UP WITH SOCIAL SECURITY IN ILLINOIS?

Most Illinois sworn personnel do not participate in Social Security for their public safety work. Chicago employees, most suburban and downstate police and fire, the State University police and, Cook County all do not participate in Social Security. But most of these people will earn a Social Security check from their non-sworn work before, during (part-time), and after their police and fire careers. The monthly check that these workers will receive from Social Security will be lower than the benefits paid to typical civilian employees. This is because these cops and firefighters spend twenty-plus years of their peak earning time outside of the Social Security system.

WHY ARE MOST ILLINOIS FIRE AND POLICE OUTSIDE OF SOCIAL SECURITY?

Pretend that you could travel back to 1787 Philadelphia. You would observe thirteen guys sitting around a table at Independence Hall banging out a draft of what would become the US Constitution. A big issue then was the relationship between the federal and state governments. Nobody wanted the federal level to be superior. After the debate was over, the national government was given some express and strongly implied powers, and the rest were left to the states explicitly or generally under the 10th Amendment.

It seems kind of quaint and outdated now, given that the national government can use highway money to get the states to change speed limits. But this concept of *federalism* is still a guiding principle of our country; the national government and the states are both sovereign and draw their powers from a constitution. Affairs within a state are generally left to the state.

Does this have anything to do with the fact that Des Plaines firefighters don't pay into Social Security? Actually, yes. When SSA was established, state and local government employees were excluded from participating due to concerns about constitutionality. The employer-employee relationship was considered to be purely a state affair (and thus beyond the role of the national government). Also, the employer "match" under FICA was seen as a tax on one level of government by another.

In time, constitutional concerns abated and amendments to SSA allowed the states to participate if the employee group was not covered by a stand-alone retirement system. Eventually each of the fifty states entered into agreements with the Social Security Administration that defined who would or would not be covered by Social Security.

In Illinois, Chicago employees were excluded from SSA participation, along with the Article 3 and 4 police/fire systems (so-called "Downstate"), the state university public safety workers, and Cook County. Departments in small towns under 5,000 in population who participated in the Illinois Municipal Retirement Fund (IMRF) were placed in Social Security. Some of those small towns eventually became big towns, established their own police or fire fund, and left the IMRF. But they maintained their participation in Social Security as part of that deal. Other communities entered into something called a 218 agreement to participate in Social Security for all employees.

THREE COPS WALK INTO A BAR...

After a regional training program, three police officers stop for a cold one to let traffic clear. One officer is from Skokie. He is covered by an Illinois Article 3 "downstate" police pension and is not in Social Security for his police work. One cop is from Algonquin. He also has Article 3 pension coverage but is *in* Social Security. The reason is that when the 1950's deal was cut with SSA, Algonquin was a small town protected by a few officers. They were too small to have established a police pension system so they were put in Social Security. But today it's a full-blown city with a police pension fund. Because of the Illinois/SSA deal, he and his coworkers are *in* Social Security forever. The third officer is from Bedford Park. She is in IMRF due to the population of that community and is also *in* Social Security.

What's the point of this bar story? History has created circumstances where the municipal police and fire responding to the same mutual aid disaster may have different pension plans or Social Security participation. A little odd, but true.

SOCIAL SECURITY BASICS

Social Security was established in 1935 as part of the New Deal legislation following the Great Depression. By 2023, it was paying just over $1.4 trillion in annual benefits; the largest program in the federal budget. The system provides base-level retirement, disability, and survivor benefits to most American workers. It is sometimes referred to as a social insurance program, intended to keep people above the poverty level. Social Security is funded by employee contributions from the paycheck, an employer match of the same amount, and taxation on Social Security benefits. The long-term projections for funding of the system show a need for improvement either in revenue (higher taxes), a larger contribution base, benefit modifications, or some combination of the three. Private, individual-accounts as a future for Social Security have been discussed but not received favorably.

In the future, even if the Social Security trust fund balance drops to zero, worker and employer contributions and taxes would cover approximately 79% of future benefits. This is certainly a gap that America can manage. It's not productive for people to proclaim that *"Social Security is not going to be there for me."* It will be.

The Basics—Who Pays for Social Security?

Workers pay 6.2% of their covered earnings for Social Security benefits and 1.45% for Medicare. Their employer matches those same payments. Wages over a certain level ($176,100 in 2025) are not taxed but are also not included in any benefit calculation. All workers, including those not in SSA, pay the 1.45% Medicare tax if they were hired after March 21, 1986. Virtually all Illinois fire and police are paying for Medicare and will be entitled to that retiree medical benefit when they turn 65.

You've seen the Social Security deduction taken out of your paycheck when you worked in SSA covered employment. It appears under the heading "FICA." This stands for Federal Insurance Contribution Act, the part of the Social Security legislation that sanctions the payroll deductions.

The Basics—How Does Someone Earn a Benefit?

You are eligible for a Social Security benefit after you earn forty "credits" in the system. A credit is earned by receiving a certain amount of Social Security covered wages in a year. In 2025, the amount was $1,810 for one credit (it was lower in the past, will be higher in the future). Up to four credits can be earned in one year, so the requirement is sometimes called "forty quarters" as opposed to "forty credits." Forty quarters is almost 100% accurate, but it's true that a school teacher on a summer break could make a little over $7,200 and earn four credits during a single calendar quarter.

Two general truths result from this. First, it takes ten years of elapsed time in Social Security to earn a benefit. Second, it's not that hard to qualify for at least a small benefit. Even if you are out of SSA for thirty years in law enforcement or fire protection, there is still time before, during and after that to earn a small amount of SSA-covered wages and get your forty quarters/credits. Most people in Illinois public safety are entitled to or are on track to be entitled to Social Security benefits. You can tell if you have earned a benefit if you received a statement from Social Security telling you so. These statements are sent to participants at age 60 but are available online before and after that age if you have registered a personal "my Social Security" account at ssa.gov.

The Basics—What Benefits are Earned?

Social Security benefits are paid to recipients, generally, in one of four forms:

- *Retirement* benefits from a worker's own record of Social Security earnings
- *Spousal* benefits from a spouse's record while the spouse is still alive
- *Survivor* benefits from a spouse's record after the spouse has died
- *Disability* benefits if you can no longer work due to illness or injury

It is important to note that a recipient may only receive one type of benefit at any one point in time. A person who receives a Survivor benefit gives up his or her own retirement benefit. A public pension fund does not work this way. If a married couple are both retired Article 3 Downstate police retirees, when one dies the survivor may receive a survivor pension as well as her own retirement pension.

BEYOND THE BASICS—RETIREMENT BENEFITS FROM YOUR OWN EARNINGS RECORD

Let's look first at how Social Security retirement benefits are calculated using the worker's own record of earnings under Social Security. This is the way that most Social Security benefits are paid, as opposed to disability, spousal and survivor benefits.

Replacement Rates, Final Salary, and Social Security

Remember your police or fire pension formula. Your benefit is calculated based on the salary at the end of your career, which is then multiplied by a percentage factor based on your years of work. This percentage is called the "replacement rate" (*i.e.*, the portion of your salary that is replaced by your pension). So 75% of final pay for thirty years of service, 50% for twenty years of service, or 65% for line-of-duty disability reflect replacement rates of 75%, 50%, and 65% respectively multiplied by final pay.

Social Security uses the same concept with two fairly major deviations. The first difference is how the salary for the computation is determined. The second is that varying replacement rates are used on different portions of your earnings. It's a bit complicated, but understandable.

Salary Used for Social Security Calculation

In the Illinois Article 3 and 4 police/fire systems, the salary used for the Tier 1 pension calculation is the salary attached to the rank on the date of retirement. For a Tier 2 member, it is the highest consecutive 48 months. In Social Security, it is the highest 35 years; *almost the entire working life of a person.* But, because some of those wages were earned so long ago, the Social Security formula adjusts (*i.e.*, indexes) those wages to inflation. Thus, if a person who retired in 2024 earned $10,000 back in 1989, Social Security indexes those wages forward to $26,916 when they calculate the person's average indexed earnings over his or her 35-year total.

A notable truth, especially for fire and police personnel: calendar years with no SSA earnings count when calculating the average earnings. Consequently, if a worker had inflation adjusted earnings of $15,000 yearly for five years, then no Social Security earnings during a 30-year public safety career ($0), then $50,000 annually for ten years, his or her average indexed earnings over the highest 35 years would be as follows:

10 years at $50,000	$500,000
5 years at $15,000	$75,000
20 years at $0	$0
Total—Highest 35 Years	$575,000
Average over 35 Years	$16,430
Indexed Monthly Average – 35 yrs	$1,369

Replacement Rates

After the average salary is calculated (called "average indexed monthly earnings" or AIME), the SSA system then uses different replacement rates for up to three separate levels of an individual retiree's indexed income. For persons attaining age 62 in 2025, those income levels and replacement rates are:

First $1,226 in monthly earnings	**90%***
Next $6,165 in monthly earnings	32%
Over $7,391 to taxable maximum	15%

Let's look at an example of how these rates work for three different Social Security recipients:

Monthly Average Wage	Calculation	Benefit	Replacement Rate
Retiree #1—$800	$800 @ 90%	$720	90%*
Retiree #2—$1,600	$1,226 @ 90% $374 @ 32%	$1,223	76%
Retiree #3—$8,500	$1,226 @ 90% $6,165 @ 32% $1,109 @ 15%	$3,242	38%

*This percentage was 40% under the repealed WEP.

Notice the progressive nature of Social Security benefits (lower income earnings receive a higher percentage replacement). The very low paid worker gets 90% of pay in Social Security benefit. The highest paid worker shown gets some at 90%, most at 32%, and a portion at 15%. The highest wage earner's final replacement rate is 38%. That 38% doesn't appear anywhere in the published formulas—it's a weighted compilation of the three different published rates of 90, 32, and 15 percent.

Estimating Your Own Benefit

What does this mean for an Illinois firefighter or police officer? For those of you who are in Social Security as a first-responder, you will earn Social Security benefits that are close to those in the example of the higher paid individuals in the prior chart.

For those of you who are not in Social Security for your police-fire career, your Average Indexed Monthly Earnings in the Social Security system will likely be quite low, and your benefit will be correspondingly low. Using the example of a person with lifetime index earnings of $1,369 shown on page 50, the Social Security benefit amounts to $1,149 at the Full Retirement Age (more on the FRA later). If you earned higher average earnings during your working life in Social Security, your benefits will be higher. Earn less than that amount, the benefit will be lower.

A superior approach is for everyone to go to the *ssa.gov* website and register for an account for access to their own private information. Once you have registered, you can examine your own record and run projections based on your earnings to-date and your estimated Social Security earnings in the future.

The good news is that since the Windfall Elimination Provision (WEP) has now been repealed, your opportunity to estimate your own Social Security benefits is the same as every other worker. Previously it was necessary to download your earnings record from ssa.gov and then input the data into a special WEP Calculator. That is no longer needed.

SOCIAL SECURITY BENEFITS FROM YOUR LIVING SPOUSE'S RECORD

In general, a retiree receives Social Security benefits equal to (a) the benefits earned from his own work record or (b) one-half of his spouse's Social Security benefit, whichever is higher. Two examples follow:

Mark's SSA Benefit	$2,000
Sue's SSA Benefit from her own record	$800
Sue will receive the following:	
From her own record	$800
From Mark's Record	$200
Sue's Total Benefit	**$1,000**

Sue is entitled to her own SSA benefit plus a spouse's benefit so that her total Social Security payment is one-half of Mark's. Together, the couple will receive $3,000 (Sue's share does not come out of Mark's benefit). A second example:

Ward's Benefit	$2,200
June's SSA Benefit from her own record	$0
June will receive the following:	
From her own record	$0
From Ward's Record	$1,100
June's Total Benefit	**$1,100**

June was at home taking care of her two sons and never worked enough time in SSA covered employment to accumulate forty credits, so she has no benefit on her own record. But she is still entitled to benefits from Ward's record of earnings. Together the couple will receive $3,300.

The Government Pension Offset (GPO)—REPEALED

Previously, the Government Pension Offset provided for a reduction in Social Security benefits *from a spouse's record* of 66-cents for every dollar an Illinois sworn employee received from a state or municipal pension if he or she was not in Social Security at the police or fire department. At the time, examples weren't really needed since the GPO usually eliminated any benefit payable under a living spouse's record.

But, as noted, the GPO has now been repealed. An Illinois police officer of firefighter may receive an unreduced Spousal benefit if his or her own earned benefit is less than one-half of the spouse's Social Security benefit.

Is a Spousal Benefit Helpful for an Illinois Police Officer or Firefighter?

The advantages of the now unrestricted Spousal benefit will vary among Illinois first-responders. For those of you who are in Social Security at your public safety job, there is no advantage. Your own Social Security benefit will be higher than one-half of your spouse's, even if she or he was a tech executive and paid the maximum in Social Security taxes.

For those of you who are outside of Social Security for most of your career, there may or may not be an advantage. If your spouse was a full-time parent for many years and earned only a modest Social Security benefit on her earnings, your own benefit will likely be more than one-half of hers (even though you were outside the Social Security system for decades). This would leave no Spousal benefit available for you.

However, if your spouse worked mostly full-time in Social Security covered employment, one-half of his or her benefit may be a little more, somewhat more or *much* more than your own Social Security. Under those circumstances, a Spousal benefit will be advantageous for you. The good news is that the Social Security application processes examines both benefits, your own and any Spousal benefit, that you may be entitled to.

SOCIAL SECURITY BENEFITS AS A SURVIVING SPOUSE

In retirement, a surviving spouse can collect up to 100% of the late spouse's Social Security benefit. There are also Survivor benefits available prior to retirement, with age and/or dependent child rules that apply. About 3.8 million widows and widowers were receiving Survivor benefits as of August 2024 (source: AARP).

However, in retirement, a surviving spouse gives up his or her own Social Security benefit once a Survivor benefit is paid. This is different than a public pension system. If a married couple consists of two retired Chicago police officers, when one dies the other can continue the retirement pension and be paid the 50% survivor benefit from the CPD pension plan. Not so with Social Security.

Previously, just like the Spousal benefit, the Government Pension Offset provided for a reduction in Social Security *Survivor* benefits. **This rule no longer applies.** It is now more likely that an Illinois police or fire professional will receive a Social Security Survivor benefit than before, but is not guaranteed. Remember that if your own Social Security benefit is higher than your wife or husband's, no Survivor benefit will be paid to you because your own benefit is higher.

A WORD ABOUT DIVORCE

Both Spousal and Survivor benefits are available based on the earnings record of an ex-spouse as long as the marriage lasted 10 years and the recipient remains unmarried. This is a special circumstance and should be personally explored if it may affect you. However, at the time of retirement, the Social Security application process should bring this opportunity into the calculation of a Spousal or Survivor benefit.

A WORD ABOUT DISABILITY BENEFITS

In addition to retirement and survivor benefits, Social Security also provides disability benefits. For police and fire personnel who are covered under Social Security at work, this may provide for a substantial increase in income if you become disabled while actively working. The benefit is essentially the Social Security benefit you would have received at the Full Retirement Age had you continued to work.

For police and fire personnel who are in Social Security at work, these benefits could prove to be substantial. However, the definition of disability under Social Security is harder to meet than the definition under the Illinois Article 3-4 police or fire pension system. This is appropriate. A firefighter who can't throw a ladder or a police officer who can't run after a fleeing suspect is disabled from public safety work and should receive a pension. But if that same person has the education, skills and abilities to perform other, non-physical work, then Social Security will not consider them to be disabled. Disability benefits from Social Security are not a sure thing even if your local pension board finds you disabled under Articles 3 or 4 of the Pension Code.

For personnel who are not in Social Security while working at the firehouse or police station, there could be a disability benefit payable to you under Social Security if you (a) meet the Social Security definition of disabled and (b) have had Social Security covered wages within a timeframe established by Social Security. If you qualify, the SSA benefit will be fairly small since your earnings exclude your professional wages. Still, that small monthly disability check could still provide a person with critical income at a time when it is sorely needed.

SOME WORDS ABOUT CLAIMING STRATEGIES

Whether or not you are in or out of Social Security for your public safety job, all of us will be faced with decisions regarding when and how to receive our Social Security benefit. There is a fancy phrase for this—a claiming strategy. This concept has been touched on in previous editions of this book. It was always an important subject, but with the repeal of the Government Pension Offset, there are now more claiming possibilities for Illinois fire and police personnel.

At the simple end of the spectrum is the issue of what age to begin taking the benefit. A retiree can begin as early as age 62 (with some limits on allowable wage income) or may defer as late as age 70. With each month of delay, the benefit goes up. A retiree and spouse might make different decisions on the age at which to draw SSA benefits. In this approach, some income starts to flow into the household but some is deferred to a later age (with the money growing each year it is deferred).

The information that follows touches on some of the basic information needed to develop a claiming strategy. Neither IPPFA nor the authors are experts in this subject, and advice on how to access the necessary expertise will follow.

Full Retirement Age (FRA)

The FRA is the age at which the calculated benefit (shown in the prior charts and examples) is payable to the retiree. In Social Security parlance this is called the Primary Insurance Amount (PIA). Your Full Retirement Age is shown on the following chart:

YEAR BORN	FULL RETIREMENT AGE
Thru 1954	66 years old, 0 months
1955	66 years old, 2 months
1956	66 years old, 4 months
1957	66 years old, 6 months
1958	66 years old, 8 months
1959	66 years old, 10 months
1960 and later	67 years old

Claiming Before your Full Retirement Age

You can claim your Social Security benefit as early as age 62. If you claim before your Full Retirement Age, the benefit is reduced each month that you draw before your FRA. Examples of the reduction amount based on an FRA of 67 years old follow:

CLAIMING AGE	REDUCTION
62	30.0%
63	24.9%
64	20.0%
65	13.1%
66	6.7%

In addition to experiencing a reduction in the monthly payment, persons who draw their Social Security before their Full Retirement Age are subject to an annual limit on wages and self-employment income. If the retiree exceeds the limit, their Social Security is reduced in a following year by 50-cents for every $1 that the limit was exceeded. In 2025 that annual wage limit is $23,400. This is an indexed amount so it will be higher in years after 2025. Note that the income limit is higher in the one year that you actually reach the FRA.

Deferring Social Security

You may also defer your retirement benefit after your Full Retirement Age. If you do so, your benefit goes up each month by a uniform increase of 8% per year (prorated monthly). Examples based on an FRA of 67 follow:

CLAIMING AGE	INCREASE IN SOCIAL SECURITY
67	Calculated Benefit
68	8% higher
69	16% higher
70	24% higher
71 and above	No further increases

What's the Best Age to Draw?

Whether there is a "best age" or not is subject to debate. There is a lot of material written and easily available on this subject. Overall, delaying your Social Security makes sense if you are going to live longer than the average American. You will receive the higher amount for more months and years.

Generally, the formulas are "neutral" based on system-wide life expectancy. Under such neutrality, if Maddie draws at 62, Mike at 67 and Mandy at 70, they all are making a good decision if it fits their needs.

While the formulas are based on system-wide life expectancy, public employees generally have educations levels at high school or above, middle class incomes and health insurance while they are working. These are all drivers of increased life expectancy. And while police and fire are identified as individuals whose life expectancy may be shorter than others due to the physical and other stresses of the job, that is only when compared to persons in similar economic positions. Also, first-responders have passed a fairly thorough medical examination and a very arduous physical fitness test. In short, your life expectancy is likely better than that reflected in the Social Security calculations.

Also, the reduction formulas do not take gender into account. Since women live longer than men, women should consider delaying their Social Security.

One approach can be, if you need the money, then begin taking Social Security. If you don't need it, delay so that your benefit is higher in your later years and any potential Survivor benefit you leave to a spouse will be higher.

Other Claiming Considerations

There may be the opportunity for some married couples to coordinate their Social Security claiming to their advantage. One spouse can begin drawing on their own benefit and then later switch to a Spouse benefit when their spouse retires.

A more complicated issue involves a retiree applying for his or her benefit but then suspending immediate receipt. This was allowed previously, but a new law quashed this benefit claiming opportunity for anyone who wasn't 62 by January 2nd of 2016. When it was allowed, the approach permitted the spouse to begin collecting a Spousal benefit. Later, that spouse could switch to benefits under his or her own SSA record, which would have grown each year the benefit was deferred up until age 70. For Illinois sworn personnel who are in Social Security, "file and suspend" could have presented some very nice alternatives. But the opportunity is now gone for most retirees.

Serious consideration of claiming strategies is beyond the scope of this book. There is a lot written on this subject, available free online. You can also engage the services of an expert, in person or online, to run specific strategies based on your (and your spouse's) actual Social Security record. You could spend a few hundred dollars at most, but be guided to a strategy worth more than $100,000 over a couple's lifetimes.

Two services that have been examined by the authors are listed below. IPPFA does not endorse any provider, but these services appeared to be thorough and reasonable in cost. They are:

MaximizemySocialSecurity.com
This is the website of a Boston University professor and author on benefit maximization. It is recommended by Terry Savage, a nationally syndicated columnist.

SocialSecurityAdvisors.com
They provide a very complete report as well as an option to speak to an expert.

Also, if you have a personal financial advisor, that individual may have advanced software that can assist you in making a claiming decision.

SOCIAL SECURITY WRAP UP

Chapter Summary

There is a lot of information in the chapter you just read. Let's summarize where we have traveled:

Social Security benefits are based on a worker's wages over his or her working life, essentially 35 years. Forty credits (usually ten years) must be earned to obtain any benefit.

Most Illinois fire and police personnel will earn Social Security benefits from work before, during, and after their public safety careers. They will generally earn a lower benefit than their civilian counterparts because of the many high-wage years they spend outside of Social Security.

Some police and fire professionals in Illinois are in Social Security for their career work.

Prior to 2025, special rules applied to the benefit calculation of persons who earned pensions outside of Social Security covered employment. Those rules, the Windfall Elimination Provision (WEP) and the Government Pension Offset (GPO) were repealed upon adoption of the *Social Security Fairness Act.* Because of this change, there is a higher likelihood that Illinois first-responders will earn benefits under the Spousal and Survivor benefit allowances.

The "three-legged stool" of retirement income includes pension, Social Security, and personal savings. For most Illinois fire and police, the Social Security leg will be lessened by a career outside of Social Security. Their generally higher pension benefits than the civilian workforce are designed in part to make up for this lower Social Security benefit.

Is Social Security Participation Valuable?

Yes. There is always a benefit to earning Social Security covered wages. If a job opportunity presents itself, either part-time or after your police-fire retirement, there is no reason not to pay the 6.2% payroll deduction and qualify for or earn a higher monthly benefit.

This applies across the board. For a new public safety professional who only has a few years in Social Security before taking the oath, it will pay in the long run for him or her to gain forty (40) credits/quarters and qualify. For someone who has already achieved Social Security eligibility and is retiring from the police or fire department, adding to their Social Security record prior to attaining age 62 or even later will add to their retirement income.

And, as discussed above, active employment in Social Security can qualify a person or increase benefits should he or she become disabled.

SOCIAL SECURITY PUBLICATIONS

Social Security has numerous publications available for download (or audio listening) from their website, ssa.gov. A few publications that may help in providing an overall view of Social Security are listed below. Some of these publications need to be updated to remove any reference to the WEP and the GPO. If you run across these provisions, don't worry about them. Recommended publications are:

Understanding the Benefits
Publication #05-10024, January 2024
Get an overview of all Social Security programs and Medicare.

Retirement Benefits
05-10035, January 2024
Learn about Social Security retirement benefits: how you earn coverage; how to apply; how benefits are figured; and how to decide when to retire.

Your Retirement Benefit: How It is Figured
05-10070, January 2023
Learn about the formula used to calculate Social Security retirement benefits and take advantage of a worksheet to help you estimate your retirement benefits.

Disability Benefits
05-10029, March 2024
People with disabilities can get basic information on Social Security benefits.

ANYTHING ELSE?

Again, you should consider opening up an account with Social Security (ssa.gov) to at least view a statement of earnings and benefits estimates or go further to see your entire record and run your own estimates.

When you get to retirement, become your own expert on the issue of claiming strategies or find a professional online or in person to assist you.

As the Social Security Administration works to implement the *Social Security Fairness Act* (and the elimination of the WEP and GPO), persons already receiving Social Security benefits will have a heightened interest in SSA's progress on these changes.

For those of you who are not yet collecting Social Security, their systems should be able to accurately handle your application when you apply in the future.

For those of you who are already collecting, the *Act* is retroactive to December 2023. It will take time for the Social Security Administration to re-calculate your benefits and make retroactive payments. At the date of this publication, Social Security had the following information on their website:

> ***If you have previously filed for Social Security benefits and they are partially or completely offset,*** at this time, you do not need to take any action except to verify that the Social Security Administration has your current mailing address and direct deposit information if it has recently changed. Most people can do this online by accessing their personal Social Security account without calling or visiting a Social Security office.
>
> ***If you have not previously filed for Social Security benefits,*** you are receiving a public pension and you are interested in filing for benefits, you can file for benefits online at ssa.gov or schedule an appointment.

Most retired Illinois fire/police who are age-eligible for Social Security benefits have applied for and are receiving benefits. However, there will be some public employees who never applied for benefits because they did not have forty credits and their pension would have totally offset any Spousal benefit. Social Security is now recommending that they apply for benefits.

We will be watching for information from Social Security as well as the websites of organizations which have closely followed these changes. Specifically, the Illinois Retired Teachers Association (irtaonline.org) and the Texas Retired Teachers Association (trta.org) are likely to have as up-to-date information as is available. IPPFA will send out bulletins when there is news worth sharing.

Finally, good luck on making the most of your Social Security benefits upon the passage of the *Social Security Fairness Act.*

UPDATE:

Social Security advises that they will post progress information on the implementation of the Social Security Fairness Act at ssa.gov/benefits/retirement/social-security-fairness-act.html.

4 DEFERRED COMPENSATION

WHAT IS DEFERRED COMPENSATION?

When a person receives wages (*i.e.*, compensation), income taxes are withheld, and the amount earned is reported to the IRS at the end of the year.

However, sections of the Internal Revenue Code (IRC) and Illinois law allow an employee to *defer* receipt of some wages until after he or she retires. At the time these deferred wages are earned, they are neither received in the paycheck, subjected to tax withholding, nor reported as taxable to the IRS (unless a Roth option is chosen, which is explained later). The money instead is deposited into an account and invested as directed by the employee. When the accumulated dollars are ultimately received after retirement (or sooner in some cases), the withdrawal payments are then reported to the IRS as taxable distributions. This deferral of wages and taxes until after retirement is commonly referred to as deferred compensation or "deferred comp."

For most public employees, deferred compensation under IRC code Section 457 is the strongest part of the "personal savings" leg of the three-legged retirement income stool (pension, Social Security and personal savings). Your personal savings can of course include the value of your home, brokerage accounts, individual retirement accounts, investment real estate, and bank savings. But the ability to save through the paycheck on a tax-advantaged basis has made deferred compensation a large personal asset for many public employees. For this reason, and because your deferred compensation operates a little differently than your neighbor's 401(k) plan or your nurse-sister's 403(b), Section 457 savings (and the accompanying chapter on healthcare savings) is the focal point of the subject of personal savings for Illinois fire and police.

Chapter Outline

In this chapter, we will first take a look at some background information on Section 457 plans. Then, we'll "follow the money." We cover how money is put into the plan, how it is invested along the way, and how it is withdrawn to meet your goal of a secure retirement. Regarding the middle part, this is not an investment guide. There is really nothing unique about 457 investing when compared to other supplemental plans where the employee self-directs the account. But we'll still go over the basics. Then the chapter ends with hopefully good tips for you on how to proceed, along with some final enthusiasm for these excellent plans.

Legal Standing

Deferred compensation systems have evolved under legislation and IRS rulings specifically in relation to the employer of each worker. Each plan is designated by the section of the Internal Revenue Code that authorizes and governs the deferral. Section 401(k) plans, the most prominent type of deferred compensation, grew out of profit-sharing plans and have been primarily used by private sector employees in for-profit companies. Section 403(b) has been the primary plan for employees of education, scientific, and charitable organizations. These plans are found in many not-for-profit hospitals, and both public and private schools. Finally, **Section 457** plans are available to employees of state and local government and, in a modified form, to some management and professional employees of not-for-profit agencies. We'll concentrate on the government form.

HISTORY OF 457 PLANS

Prior to 1978, various organizations obtained "private letter rulings" from the IRS allowing public employees to defer compensation. An actual code section authorizing deferrals was subsequently included in the *Revenue Act of 1978* as a new Section 457(b) of the code. There have been revisions since then, the notable being the improvements in the 1996, 2000, and 2002 reform laws. Most importantly, the **1996 reform law** established that funds held in a 457 plan are trust funds and are not available to the municipalities' general creditors. This change, long overdue, followed the bankruptcy of Orange County (California) after an investment scandal.

Changes in 2000 and 2002 went a long way in making the 457 plan look just like its private sector cohorts under 401(k) and 403(b). The allowable contribution amounts were made to be very similar between the plans. The withdrawal rules and the opportunity for rollover from one plan to the other or to an Individual Retirement Account (IRA) were made similar. Prior to these reforms, it was very important for public sector employees to be given special instruction on 457 plan deferred compensation (the withdrawal rules were particularly complicated). That need has lessened now—public employees can obtain general information from the financial industry or media on deferred compensation and then check with their plan administrator for specific 457 plan rules.

HOW DOES TAX DEFERRAL IMPROVE RETIREMENT SAVINGS?

In a traditional tax-deferred plan, an employee elects to defer compensation at a set amount or a percentage of pay. When he or she is paid each payday, the deferred compensation amount is deducted from the paycheck and deposited into a special account. Taxes withheld from the paycheck are calculated on the basis that the amount deferred was taken from the paycheck "before taxes." So, the paycheck does not go down as much as the total amount put into the deferred compensation account. Then, at the end of the year, the amount deferred is not reported to the IRS or state as a taxable wage. An example follows.

A Tale of Two Savers

To see how deferring compensation compares to savings through taxable channels, let's look at two savers, Tim and Suzanne. They both earn $4,000 monthly and can afford to put away $300 per month for retirement savings. Tim opens a brokerage account for his investments and has his employer sends the $300 to his account via the ACH automated banking system. Suzanne joins her public employer's deferred compensation plan. Here's how their monthly gross and take-home pay are affected (excluding Social Security or pension contributions, which are unchanged by either approach).

	TIM	SUZANNE
Salary	$4,000	$4,000
Deferred Compensation	0	(428)
Taxable Wages	$4,000	$3,572
Federal Tax	540	427
State Tax	200	185
Brokerage Account Deposit	300	0
Net Pay	$2,960	$2,960

Tim and Suzanne both have the same monthly net pay but Suzanne saves $428 monthly while Tim puts away only $300. This happens because Suzanne's tax deferral advantage on the $428 deposit reduces her net pay by only the $300 that she can afford. Of course, Tim is free and clear on the taxes for the principle amount he has saved; Suzanne eventually does pay the tax on her $428. But let's see how that works out.

Suppose Tim earns 7.5% annually on his savings and pays 23.1% in tax on his earnings each year. If he keeps up his savings/investment/tax program for 30 years, he'll have $281,200 in his account at retirement. If Suzanne earns the same 7.5% return over 30 years, her balance will accumulate to $551,000. She still owes tax on that amount, but she has almost twice the amount that Tim has. Tax rates are simply not high enough to take away the advantages she has already gained.

Also, there are other factors in her favor. First, if she lives in a state that doesn't tax 457 withdrawals, such as Illinois, she will avoid the state tax completely. Moreover, if she draws her money out gradually (while still experiencing investment earnings), she will continue to enjoy the benefit of tax deferral while drawing money out at levels that do not trigger excessive taxes.

Personal financial experts are virtually unanimous in their advice that deferred compensation is an excellent way to save. Even changes in the tax code, which reduced taxes for people who own stocks and mutual funds outside of deferred compensation, have not diminished the attractiveness of these plans.

NOTE

If an employee routinely pays a large amount of money to the IRS at year-end, enrolling in or increasing deferrals in a Section 457 plan may not eliminate a large tax payment on April 15th, although it will reduce it somewhat. The employee may still need to adjust his tax or her withholding by completing a revised declaration of exemptions (W-4), which is available from the payroll office.

WHAT ABOUT THE ROTH APPROACH?

There was a senator from Delaware named Roth who in 1997 got Congress to establish the Roth IRA. In time, that morphed over into a Roth 401(k) and eventually a Roth 457 option. Your employer may or may not offer a Roth 457 plan or option.

The majority of public employees save for retirement using a traditional tax-deferred 457 plan as opposed to a Roth. Because of that, we've concentrated this chapter of the book on the method that most of us have used. Also, the pros and cons of Roth savings are the same for you as for your IRA or 401(k) saving friends and relatives. So, you can get good information from most sources that provide such advice.

But, in case this Roth thing is new to you, we provide just a short explanation. In a Roth 457 plan, there is no tax savings or other advantage at the time the employee makes his or her payroll deduction deposit. So if Suzanne in my example put $428 monthly into a Roth 457 plan, her pay would go down $428, not the $300 shown in the table. However, the money earned on Roth deposits is not taxed at the time of withdrawal. So the earnings in a Roth account are not simply tax-deferred, they are *tax-exempt*—a much better tax treatment.

Both during employment and afterward, there is an opportunity to convert money deposited under the tax-deferred approach over to a Roth arrangement. This involves a modestly sophisticated effort to measure the impact of today's tax rates versus future rates (although there is no prediction regarding the present Illinois income tax—retirement income including deferred compensation is not taxed). The IPPFA benefits division reports that some active participants use the option of an "in-plan Roth conversion" to move money deposited with a tax advantage over to Roth treatment. You can work with your tax advisor and/or deferred compensation plan to evaluate these options.

To summarize, the Roth has no tax break at the time of the deposit, but *all* of the earnings are tax-exempt. Not just deferred, *exempt*. The traditional 457 approach gives the saver a tax break going in, essentially creating more money to be saved, but those tax-deferred deposits and all earning are eventually taxed.

RULES FOR DEFERRING INCOME

A maximum of $23,500 may be deferred in 2025, which will be indexed to inflation in the future. There is no statutory minimum amount of deferral. Some administrators or employers may set a minimum, say $10 or 1% of pay. Your employer's payroll system may support either a flat deferral or a percentage of wages or both. An advantage to deferring based on a percentage is that if you work overtime or get a pay raise or promotion, some of that increased salary is deferred automatically without any action on your part.

There is a provision of Section 457 that allows an employee to exceed the annual maximum, up to double the amount of the annual maximum, in the last three years prior to being eligible to receive a pension from the employer-sponsored retirement plan. The additional amount deferred is limited to amounts that the employee *could* have legally deferred in the past but did not. It is further limited to the annual amount for regular contributions. For example, if the employee could have deferred $7,500 in each year of his first ten years of employment ($75,000) but only deferred $45,000 during those years, he or she has $30,000 left that can be deferred in the last three years prior to eligibility for receipt of pension (in addition to the regular maximum).

This extra allowance is nicknamed **"the Catch-up Provision,"** since the employee is catching-up on deferrals that could have been made earlier in his career.

The 2000 reform law added an additional savings opportunity, the so-called "Age 50 Catch-up Provision." This provision allowed a person over age 50 to contribute an additional $1,000 in 2002, incrementally increasing to $7,500 in 2025. This additional amount cannot be contributed in a year when the standard Catch-up Provision is being used. This Age 50 allowance is not dependent upon the existence of "unused deferrals" in prior years. It is simply additional authority to defer salary.

And now, under a new retirement law called SECURE 2.0, the IRS has announced an increased contribution limit in 2025 for those ages 60-63. This additional catchup rule allows someone who qualifies to contribute an additional $11,250 to the standard contribution limit of $23,500. To qualify for the enhanced catch-up contributions, participants must meet specific criteria: be age 60, 61, 62, or 63 by the end of the calendar year and generally already contributed the maximum deferral amount. This catch-up allows for a total contribution of $34,750 for 2025. Note that once participants turn 64, they revert to the standard Age 50+ catch-up contribution limit. And some good news, the amount of this SECURE 2.0 enhanced catch-up may increase in future years as it is indexed to the Age 50+ catch-up allowance.

THE RULE OF 72

Catch-up provisions are okay. But, if you can afford to, it's so much better to put a little more money into deferred compensation during your career than a lot of money at the end. Let's explore that idea further and learn an important investment concept along the way.

The variables that effect how much you accumulate in deferred compensation are the amount you put in, your investment return, and how long the money stays on deposit. The time factor is huge. The longer the amount of time your money is on deposit, the more fantastic things happen to it.

There is a mathematical **Rule of 72.** An investor can take his or her expected rate of investment earnings and divide it into 72. The product of that division is the length of time in years that it will take the invested money to double in value. So, at an easy-to-use estimate of 7.2% annual investment return, money doubles every ten years (72 divided by 7.2% = 10 years). If $3,000 is invested, it will become $6,000 in ten years, $12,000 in twenty years and $24,000 in thirty years. If the rate of earnings is higher, say at 8%, money will then double every nine years, not ten. At thirty years the same deposits will have grown to not $24,000 but $30,000.

The Rule of 72 also amplifies the importance of time. If a person made that same $3,000 investment three years earlier and had it on deposit for thirty-three years, the same one-time deposit of $3,000 at 8% will grow to $38,000—26% more than the same dollars invested for thirty years.

Remember Suzanne's accumulated $551,000. Say she increases her savings in the last three years by a total of $30,000 by "catching up" $10,000 each year. If she does this, her end-of-thirty-year total grows to $584,000. If she instead found a way to put in the additional $30,000 by saving $1,000 more in each of the thirty years of her participation, the balance at the end is $658,000. True story.

Time is your friend. Save as much as you reasonably can as early as you can. Capitalize on "The Rule of 72."

BUT YOU MAY WANT TO CATCH-UP TO SAVE STATE TAXES

Although the Catch-up Provisions aren't hugely effective for long term savings, there is a short-term advantage: money withdrawn from Section 457 plans in Illinois is not subject to state taxes. So, a participant can save 4.95% on his or her money going into the plan (since it's not subject to Illinois withholding or reporting) but state taxes are not assessed on the money when it is withdrawn. Thus, state taxes are not just deferred, they are eliminated completely. This is true on all your deferred compensation deposits and earnings if you remain an Illinois taxpayer and the law is not changed.

DEFERRED COMPENSATION—INVESTMENT OVERVIEW

This is an area in which you are not different. Any book, article or advice from an expert that educates you about asset allocation for retirement savings works for Section 457 plans.

Like the 401(k) plan, most Section 457 administrators offer a variety of investments in the form of either public mutual funds or commingled investment accounts managed by investment experts. A participant is able to select from fixed or guaranteed rate investment accounts, various stock accounts, government and/or corporate bond accounts, a money-market account, or blended or balanced accounts that offer a combination of stocks, bonds, and short-term investment instruments. Your investment is held in trust and can only be used for your benefit under the rules of the plan and the Internal Revenue Code.

Since you can get advice or information anywhere and your investment goals and selections are not any different than your neighbor with a 401(k) plan, this book is not an investment guide. But we'll go over the basics, plus you may well have a certain amount of financial acumen anyway. You can then decide how much more research or assistance you need, if any, on this aspect of your personal savings and retirement plan.

WHO BELONGS IN WHAT INVESTMENT?

Professional investors break down the types of investments into broad asset classes—stocks, bonds, real estate, commodities, *etc*. How those are mixed together in a portfolio is called **asset allocation**. How does one select an asset allocation that is right for his or her long-term goals? You need to spend some time on this, as the experts say that asset allocation decision is far more important than which individual investments or funds that you select.

The American economic system rewards ownership. It is more advantageous to own a company than to lend the company (or a government) money, although lending certainly has its place in the economy and as an investment. When you invest in a stock mutual fund or other type of stock account, you are taking partial ownership of the many companies in the account. So, it is not a surprise that, by all historic measurements, stock market investments outperform other asset classes. Accordingly, the percent of your asset allocation that you have in the stock market should be a key consideration.

The reality of investment returns supports the philosophical view of the benefits of ownership. Here are the various domestic market returns from January 1st, 1926 (before the Great Depression) to December 31, 2023:

ASSET CLASS	ANNUAL RETURN
Small Company Stocks	11.8%
Large Company Stocks	10.3%
Long Government Bonds	5.1%
30-Day US Treasury Bills	3.3%

Source Ibbotson SSBI

Of course, such returns and those in the future may come with great volatility. Just look at what we've experienced over the past two decades: fantastic highs, retractions, periods of steady returns, two huge drops, and then big recoveries. But if you are a long term investor, the long-term returns in stocks beat the safer bets, as long as you take some effort to manage the volatility.

PUBLIC EMPLOYEES ARE AGGRESSIVE INVESTORS

Both from the records of the IPPFA benefits division and anecdotally from other workers, we see that public employees tend to be fairly aggressive in their deferred compensation investing. That is, they have a relatively high percentage of their asset allocation in the stock market. They thus often capture more of the gains possible, as indicated in the preceding chart.

Whether these investors are less risk-adverse than the average investor or maybe just smarter, underlying this trend is a valid long-term saving concept. Because public employees are more likely to have a pension, *i.e.*, a guaranteed retirement income (as opposed to a more volatile 401(k) arrangement), they can take more risk with their separate, personal retirement saving.

100% MINUS YOUR AGE

If you prefer to be a little less aggressive, some personal financial experts suggest a basic formula known as **100% minus your age**. If you follow this formula, the percentage of your retirement assets that you will have in equities (*i.e.*, the stock market) will be equal to 100% minus your age. For example, if a person is 45 years old and subtracts his age from 100, the difference of 55 (*i.e.*, 55%) represents a suggested level for him to invest in stocks. If he was deferring $100 per paycheck, $55 would go to stocks and the balance would go to the bond or fixed accounts.

Using this formula, or a similar approach, a saver ends up investing more aggressively when he or she is younger. At age 22, "100% minus your age" puts 78% of money in stocks. Continuing, the formula reduces stock holdings as a person ages and ultimately approaches retirement. At age 60, only 40% of the money will be in stocks. This is what you may want to happen, because the amount of the portfolio that is in a volatile investment is reduced as retirement approaches. But you still maintain some opportunity for growth to beat inflation or a hopefully long life. Under this approach, even an octogenarian has 20% of her retirement account in the stock market.

WHY NOT 100% IN STOCKS?

If stocks always beat everything else, why not put 100% in stocks? You may want to. But remember that we can go through prolonged periods of stock market downturns.

Here is another math lesson. If I have a $1,000 stock investment that drops 25%, what do I have left? The answer is $750. This isn't too hard to figure out. But here is an important follow up question. What investment return do I then need to get my $750 back to $1,000 before I can grow my initial investment even by one penny? The answer is 33%, not the 25% I originally lost. Volatility is not just your investment going up and down—*volatility can hurt your returns.* That's why a 100% allocation to stock may be a little too risky.

Also, when the market is down for a prolonged period, your fixed income investments will help you keep your balances up *and* reinforce your confidence in deferred compensation. Further, placing a small portion of a portfolio in another asset class, even one that does not perform as well as your core investments, can result in less volatility and higher earnings if the account is rebalanced from time to time (more on that to follow).

Both of these factors is where the phase **diversification** comes in; you've heard that before. A variety of asset classes in your diversified portfolio keeps you almost whole when one asset class underperforms. You also have the opportunity to rebalance between the asset classes to your long-term benefit.

REBALANCING

Very importantly, an allocation to both stocks and fixed income which you regularly rebalance will give you the opportunity to actually "buy low, sell high" for a long-term overall gain.

Let's say firefighter Addie is an avid deferred compensation investor and currently deposits her money each payday along a 60/40 stock/bond mix, with some of the stock piece in small companies and foreign stocks, and some of the fixed income piece to the plan's stable value fund. Over time, thanks to the pretty good performance in all aspects of her stock allocation, her account balance looks like this:

Small Company Stocks	$16,000	13%
Foreign Stocks	$8,000	6%
S&P 500 Index Fund	$59,000	46%
Bond Fund	$34,000	26%
Stable Value Fund	$11,000	9%
	$128,000	100%

Addie's stock allocation is now 65% of her portfolio even though her deposits went in at 60%. Good for her! She has been rewarded for her allocation to stocks. But she truly likes that 60/40 mix as part of her long-term goals and volatility management, so she rebalances the portfolio to look like this:

Small Company Stocks	$12,800	10%
Foreign Stocks	$6,400	5%
S&P 500 Index Fund	$57,600	45%
Bond Fund	$38,400	30%
Stable Value Fund	$12,800	10%
	$128,000	100%

She has been disciplined at rebalancing, and transferred 5% of her money out of stocks and into bonds or fixed income investments, bringing her balance to the target 60/40 mix (as well as to her specific desired allocations within all stock and fixed income asset classes). Now, if the stock market or a specific portion of it drops, she has already captured some gains by transferring money out of stocks to bonds when stock values were higher.

Likewise, after the stock market has a bad year, she will rebalance bond money over to the stock side of her portfolio at the time that stocks are "cheap." Then when stocks recover, she will have more invested in stocks at the beginning of the rally.

A study published in *Forbes* in 2011 examined two hypothetical investors who each put $10,000 into a 60/40 mix of stocks and bonds in 1985. One never rebalanced the portfolio, the other rebalanced annually. For the entire 25-year period from 1985 to 2010, the portfolio of the guy who rebalanced grew to $97,000, beating the other investor at $89,000. Of course, there were times when the rebalancing didn't work, such as a prolonged bull market in stocks. But the theory and the practice over the decades supported the concept of rebalancing a portfolio.

There are "balanced" funds in some 457 plans that automatically rebalance to their targets. And some plans have a feature where you can mark your account to rebalance itself at some interval. Or you can keep your eyes on your account and rebalance on a set schedule or just make a judgment call when you get a little or a lot off target.

This section closes with an anecdote from the Skokie Police Pension Fund. In February of 2009 SPD pension rebalanced the portfolio back to the then 45% target in stocks after taking a beating in the market but holding firm on their investment philosophy and policy. They rebalanced just in time to catch the great stock market rebound that began in March 2009. Other local police and fire funds likely had similar experiences.

ASSET ALLOCATION AND REBALANCING MADE EASY

A generation ago an investment adviser could conduct a two-day seminar on the why's and how's of proper asset allocation, diversification, and rebalancing. Then the major mutual fund companies and plan administrators came along with new products that execute these strategies automatically—the "balanced fund" or the "target date" fund or something similar. Balanced funds invest in a blend of assets that is routinely rebalanced. In a target date fund, the investor picks an approximate date for retirement, say 2050, then invests in a fund with that 2050 retirement goal in mind. That investment fund in 2021 is fairly aggressive in terms of its allocation to equities (stocks), including higher risk small companies and foreign stocks. But as 2050 approaches, the manager switches gradually to a more conservative portfolio. And, along the way, the account is regularly rebalanced.

As long as the fees charged are reasonable (always watch fees), this is a great way to save.

A WORD ABOUT PASSIVE INVESTING

If you don't choose a target date fund but prefer to select your own investments, a well-regarded piece of advice is to invest some or a good portion of your savings in an index fund. Let's examine the idea of an "index" and then explore the concept and advantages of an index fund.

An **index** is a hypothetical portfolio of investments that a knowledgeable group of people believe properly reflects the performance of an entire asset class. We hear about indexes all the time. When the TV news reports that the stock market went up 40 points, what does that mean? It means that a stock index, usually 30 companies monitored by the Dow Jones Company, went up 40 points. A broader index from Standard & Poors tracks 500 large-company stocks; it is called the S&P 500 Index. When the stock market is measured over the years and decades, most observers are talking about the S&P 500. And there is an index for almost every asset class.

In 1976, the first "stock index fund" was launched, in which investor money was simply placed in each of the 500 S&P stocks. The fund did not have stock analysts researching whether any one stock, say IBM, was good deal. IBM was in the index, so it was in the investment fund. Continuing, the index fund manager didn't consult economists to predict the ups and downs of the energy crisis. If 17% of the S&P 500 index companies were energy-related, then 17% of the index fund was in energy.

This is sometimes called **passive investing**. That phrase is used to differentiate the investment approach from an "active" manager who studies interest rates, company credit ratings, economic growth, and a zillion other factors before making an investment. The "passive" manager just sits back passively and selects securities that are in the underlying index.

This started in 1976. Today, there are trillions of dollars in index funds of all types: S&P 500, Wilshire 3000 small company index, Barclay's aggregate bond index, and many others.

Why invest in index funds? For two reasons: First, it's cheap. The fees charged against your investment balance in an index fund are the lowest available (your returns in public employee deferred compensation are always "net" of the fees paid to the investment manager). Since the index manager doesn't have to hire analysts and economists for the fund, those savings are passed on to the investor. Secondly, stock index funds, over time, produce returns comparable to or exceeding the more expensive "active" management approach.

But you may do better using active managers. Just keep the index concept in mind and do your own research into index or passive investing if the matter interests you.

HOW SAFE IS SECTION 457 INVESTING?

Risk of loss of principle is always present unless you are directly buying US government bonds or making FDIC insured bank deposits. Everything else includes some risk, such as a company going out of business or a foreign government defaulting on its debt. Only you can do both the research and the self-analysis to decide how much risk you are willing to take. The good news is that the various types of investment risk—credit, market, interest rates, foreign currency, whatever—are unchanged inside the Section 457 umbrella. Investing in the Vanguard Life Strategy Income Fund directly or through your 457 plan is no different, risk or otherwise.

How about out-and-out theft? Remember Bernie Madoff. He took investors' money, did *not* buy the securities or options that he promised, and then created phony statements to indicate that he had made proper investments. Meanwhile he was living the good life on his investors' cash. Could that happen in a major 457 administrator's operation or in the underlying mutual funds or accounts? Never say never, but it's just highly unlikely. All these operations have the proper trust account and custodian players in place (a custodian is a bank that holds the investments—the investment manager does not have access to the actual securities). If you have any doubts, talk to your plan representative.

Could a 457 plan choose an insurance company for a guaranteed investment contract (GIC) and have that company go bankrupt? Yes, it could, but there is a higher chance that this would happen if you did it yourself. And those GIC monies are usually protected by state guarantee funds.

We have a lot of confidence that the assets are safe. We know of no money that has been lost in modern day 457 savings other than from routine and expected investment volatility.

CLOSING THOUGHTS ON INVESTING

Deferred compensation plans give a public employee the opportunity to build a diversified portfolio with an amazingly small starting investment. For example, a new participant in deferred compensation might have his or her first $20 deposit put one-fourth each into an S&P 500 index fund, a small company stock fund, an international stock fund, and a government bond fund. Is this really possible with just $20: a $5 investment into foreign stocks and the rest into a diversified stock and bond portfolio? Yes, it is possible—in employer-sponsored deferred compensation.

Allocation of retirement investment among asset classes is your most important decision after the decision to save, and before the decision of which specific mutual funds to pick. If you are unsure of how to invest your money, do some research or seek investment advice from a professional. Investing in a 457 plan is very similar to investing in a 401(k) plan, so investment advisers, good ones, should be able to help you.

A recommendation is either of two excellent books by William Bernstein: *The Intelligent Asset Allocator* and *The Four Pillars of Investing: Lessons for Building a Winning Portfolio*. Dr. Bernstein is a neurologist who at some point began to fancy himself to be an investment expert. Turned out he was right. You can use the excellent information in either of these books to assist you in your deferred compensation investment plan.

One way that a 401(k) plan and a 457 plan are dissimilar is that the 401(k) private sector employee may receive an employer match. The trade-off usually is that the private sector worker probably does not have a defined benefit pension like you do. But since you do have a DB plan, here's something to remember: your fixed pension acts in many ways like a bond investment. If you consider that when you decide on an asset allocation in deferred compensation, you'll put considerably more in the domestic and foreign stock markets. The fact that your defined benefit pension plan pays out a guaranteed fixed amount each month allows you to be more aggressive in the stock market with personal savings.

Timing the market doesn't work. If you think you can *consistently* move out of stocks at the top and go back in at the bottom of the market, get out of public safety and make yourself a billionaire.

TURNING 457 MONEY INTO RETIREMENT INCOME

Section 457 money is deferred for retirement purposes. You do not have access to the funds until you either separate from employment (quit or retire) or have an unforeseeable financial emergency. The rules regarding withdrawal for an unforeseeable emergency are very strict. The emergency must be something for which a reasonable person would not budget and cannot be dealt with using savings outside of the Section 457 plan. Imminent foreclosure, eviction, uninsured medical or funeral expenses or an uninsured casualty loss are examples of unforeseeable emergencies. *This is a high barrier to access.* Don't plan on being able to get the money until you leave the job. Deferred compensation is a supplemental *retirement plan*; consider it as such.

BEFORE YOU NEED THE MONEY, SHOULD YOU STAY WHERE YOU ARE OR USE THE IRA ROLLOVER OPTION?

At the time you retire, you may not need any of the proceeds of your Section 457 account. If you leave the money in place, your balance continues to grow on a tax-deferred basis. If you don't want to begin drawing the money at retirement, the only decision to be made is whether or not you want to leave your balance with your employer's deferred compensation plan or roll it over into an existing or new Individual Retirement Account (IRA).

There is a good case for leaving the money where it is if you are satisfied with the employer-sponsored 457 plan: the investment options that are offered, the fees, the customer service provided by the administrator, the continued oversight by your employer and union, and the opportunity to discuss the plan with your active and retired coworkers. If you are happy with the plan that helped you build a pretty good nest egg, why change?

There is a case for rolling the money into an IRA if you are not totally satisfied with your employer's plan, you'd like to consolidate your investments with another company or advisor, or you want to make some distributions to charities though an IRA permitted "Qualified Charitable Distribution (QCD)."

A word of caution is in order regarding the 10% penalty that is paid when money is withdrawn from an IRA before age 59 1/2. Your municipal 457 plan does not have a 10% penalty for withdrawal before age 59 1/2. **Whenever you take out Section 457 money you pay only the tax.** But IRAs and a new employer's 401(k) plan *do* have such a penalty. If you roll Section 457 money into a plan that has such a rule, your 457 money will be subject to a 10% penalty if withdrawn before age 59 1/2. For this reason, it might be better to leave your balance with the deferred compensation plan administrator at least until you are ready to begin distributions or at least until after age 59 1/2.

There is a lot of good information available from general sources to help you make the rollover/don't-rollover decision.

Rolling your money over into an IRA and then converting the IRA to a Roth IRA is a related strategy; again beyond the scope of this book. But there is considerable information and advice available on this subject.

WHEN YOU NEED THE MONEY

Prior to age 73, most Section 457 plan administrators and IRA custodians allow considerable flexibility on withdrawal of the funds. As retirement approaches, you should be in contact with your administrator to go over your options. Taking all your money out at once is certainly allowed. This is the so-called "lump sum option," but you'll possibly skyrocket into a high tax bracket if you do this. Not a good idea.

You may want to choose a series of systematic withdrawals paid on a set schedule (month, quarter, year). While the money is being paid out, your balance stays invested as you have directed. Your administrator might also offer the opportunity for you to start receiving one monthly amount but then receive an increasing amount each year in the future.

Or you may choose some other schedule. When that time comes, check out your options. Again, your balance always stays invested as you directed while you are drawing out the money.

There is a lot written about how much a retiree can safely draw out of a defined contribution retirement plan and not run out of money during his or her life. Since public employee deferred compensation plans are supplemental to a pension (in the case of Illinois, an inflation-adjusted pension), the rate of withdrawal is not critical as it is for a person in a 401(k)-only retirement environment. Again, there is a lot written on this subject and it is easily available.

REQUIRED MINIMUM DISTRIBUTIONS

However, beginning at age 73, if you are no longer working for the 457 sponsor, you must begin withdrawals that meet or exceed so-called Required Minimum Distributions (RMD). Essentially the RMD is an annual amount calculated with the intent that most of the account balance will be withdrawn during the remaining life of the participant. The plan administrator can advise you of how the RMD schedule will work and may have an on-line RMD Calculator to assist you in your planning. You can also look directly at the approved IRS schedule at irs.gov or simply Google "RMD table."

Here is a quick example. At the date of publication of this book, an age 73 retiree with a $200,000 account balance must withdraw at least $7,547 that year. At age 81, an account balance of $200,000 would trigger a minimum withdrawal of $10,309. These numbers will vary in the future.

If you do not live long enough to draw out a large part of your balance, there is no penalty associated with this. Any balance left when you die passes to your heirs and the tax liability is transferred to the next owner. Your beneficiary pays the tax when the money is withdrawn.

Work closely with your IRA custodian or 457 plan administrator to ensure you are in compliance with RMD rules.

THE ANNUITY OPTION

Before or after age 73, there is the opportunity to purchase an **annuity** to pay you (or you and your spouse) a monthly amount for life. Under this option, your balance does *not* stay invested as you direct. The annuity company takes all the money in exchange for the promise to pay the annuity each month as long as you live. If you live a short time, they win. If you live until 102, *you* win. There are also some variations where you can guarantee that a minimum number of payments will be made to your survivors even if you don't live a long time. Examples of specific types of payments follow later.

When you buy an annuity, you are really transferring investment risk and mortality risk (*i.e.*, how long you are going to live) to an insurance company. Some people may want to do this. If a person was self-employed and sold a business in retirement for $3 million, he or she might reasonably consider using some of that money to buy an annuity. Since that retiree does not have a pension, the annuity that is purchased acts in many ways just like a pension.

But not many public safety retirees choose annuities to withdraw money from their deferred compensation plan. They already have a guaranteed income for life (the fire or police pension) with some level of inflation protection. They likely also have a Social Security benefit coming, even if they were not covered under that federal system while working at the police or fire department. So, it's reasonably safe for a police or fire pensioner to accept the investment and mortality risk of their deferred compensation account as opposed to transferring that risk to an insurance company (and incurring the insurance contract's attendant fees and profits).

Your plan administrator can provide you with estimates of how much monthly income an annuity will pay to a retiree or a joint retiree/spouse payment. A quick public source is the website www.immediateannuities.com. At the date this book was written, that website estimated that 60-year-old police captain John and his wife, 58-year-old Kate, would receive the following monthly payment annuity options for a $200,000 deferred compensation balance:

For John's life	$863/month
For John's life, 10 years guaranteed	$851
For John or Kate's life	$718

Just like any other product purchased from an insurance company, the more protection you want the more you pay in premium (or in this case, the more you give up in monthly income). John can get $863 per month for life. If he gets hit by a bus the next year, his entire balance is gone—he forfeited it when he elected an annuity. But if he lives to 102, he'll draw more than $430,000 from his account. If he selects the 10-year guarantee and draws $851 per month, then dies at age 68, the monthly payment of $851 continues to his beneficiary for another 2 years. If he selects the $718 option, he gets that amount each month and the payments continue to Kate after he dies for as long as she lives. If she lives a long time, it may be a good deal. But, if Kate lives a short time longer or, worse, dies before John, the "insurance" was wasted.

Even if you will not be interested in an annuity, the tools at www.immediateannuities.com might be helpful because it will give you a good idea as to how much money you can withdraw from your Section 457 balance during your lifetime, and your spouse's lifetime. For example, John and Kate above could decide to keep their money invested in the police department's Section 457 plan and take a monthly check of $718. This amount will likely surpass the minimum requirement when John reaches age 72 and is an amount that the experts (the annuity company) say should last during their joint life expectancies. But at the same time, they haven't given up any rights to an annuity company or incurred annuity costs. Should they both die younger than expected, there will be a balance in their account that can be left to their eight children.

DEFERRED COMPENSATION SUMMARY

A public employee can place a considerable amount of personal savings into a deferred compensation account. This approach will beat savings outside the account over the long term. There are a broad range of diversified asset classes that can be chosen and mixed to create excellent long-term gains. Participants should understand these investments well enough to make appropriate allocation decisions. If you are not in that position, you can improve your own knowledge and/or work with the deferred compensation company or a personal advisor to assist you. Rebalancing your account regularly or even from time to time adds value. Deferred compensation accounts can also be put on a sort of "automatic pilot" as there are opportunities for preset, age-appropriate investing and rebalancing. There is a lot of flexibility in withdrawing the money, but moderately sized withdrawals must occur after age 73.

THOUGHTS THAT DIDN'T FIT ANYWHERE ELSE

Section 457 plans are very popular where they have been introduced. And, these plans were popular under the *old* rules, which restricted withdrawal options and treated account balances as the property of an employer. With the 1996 and 2000 reforms, interest in 457 plan participation grew. The tax break on contributions, access to the broad investment markets for a small deposit and the convenience of payroll deduction make these plans an excellent "third leg" of the retirement stool.

Police and fire personnel should take pride in the fact that they and their co-workers are the largest savers among public employees. This is most likely due to a tradition of taking care of each other. You depend on your coworkers at a working fire or a crime-in-progress. You look out for each other then and you look out for the young officers and firefighters by encouraging them to participate in deferred compensation. Keep up the good work.

The dollars that go into deferred compensation will end up in competition with other expense and savings needs: buying a house, saving for kids' college, and other requirements of life. It's hard to max out every year and still feed your family. So don't worry when your first child is born and your spouse cuts back at work. You will probably need to drop your contribution to deferred compensation. Keep everything in balance. But remember that magical time value of compounded earnings. Don't let deferred compensation sit too long on a back burner. The best approach: start deferring as soon as you are eligible.

WHAT ELSE CAN YOU DO TO IMPROVE YOUR DEFERRED SAVINGS?

There are a range of further actions you can consider. Or not. Many of the readers already have a good grasp of their deferred compensation personal savings plan.

Of course, if you are not saving in deferred compensation, strongly consider joining the plan. If your employer does not have a deferred compensation plan, contact your union. If you are not represented by a union, contact IPPFA to see about the IPPFA Benefits Division (NPPFA) approaching your employer.

If you are enrolled in deferred compensation and would like to improve this leg of your retirement income, you can do a little or a lot. Reread this chapter. Visit your plan administrator's website or review the written plan material. Consider the two recommended books from Dr. Bernstein or find something similar. Maybe a relative or a friend has a decent financial planning or retirement book.

Rebalance your account if it hasn't been done since the 1990s. Be sure you understand your investments and statements. If you don't understand them, plan a meeting with the deferred compensation representative. Take ownership.

ADVICE

NPPFA Benefits offers both a traditional and a Roth deferred compensation plan. For any information on deferred compensation, related to an IPPFA plan or any other plan, please feel free to contact NPPFA Benefits.

NPPFA BENEFITS

Joel Babbitt, joelb@nppfabenefits.org, 773-617-9690

Anita Kochar, anitak@nppfabenefits.org, 847-323-0219

www.nppfabenefits.org

1701 E Lake Avenue Suite 400
Glenview, IL 60025

SECTION ENDNOTES

To arrive at the 23.1% tax rate imputed for "Tim's" savings outside of deferred compensation, the following was used: a blended the capital gains/dividend rate for three-quarters of his investment earnings with a typical top rate of 28%, then added 4.95 percentage points for Illinois tax.

5 RETIREMENT HEALTHCARE FUNDING PLANS

Dan at the IPPFA Office had a special birthday a few years ago. It was the one where the federal government sends out a red, white and blue card for you to receive healthcare benefits as a reward for paying decades of Medicare taxes. Before that he was covered under his former employer's health plan. But that employment *did not* require him to respond to fires or bar fights, which was appropriate for guys his age.

IPPFA's active membership is not that lucky. They are generally going to have to retire earlier than the mid-60's and, relatedly, be exposed to some pretty significant medical premium costs until they hit Medicare age.

Illinois has enacted Public Act 86-1444 that allows certain public sector retirees to continue to participate with their employer's group health insurance plan **after retirement**. Illinois has limited, if any, employer-sponsored subsidized retiree health benefits for public safety workers. Chicago Fire and Police subsidize retiree medical, but that subsidy is decreasing. The vast majority of Illinois police and fire professionals can continue to participate with the health insurance plan upon retirement, but there is no employer contribution to the premiums. They are on their own for retiree medical coverage and costs.

This leads us to the following:

> Retiree and family healthcare costs are significant for all Americans, more so for those who leave active employment early due to the physical burdens of public safety work.
>
> Saving for retirement healthcare will be a significant portion of the "personal savings" part of the three-legged retirement stool.

On average, 45% of a pre-65 retiree's pension check is consumed between income taxes and health insurance premiums before the recipient receives the payment.

Fortunately, the Internal Revenue Code allows significant tax advantages for saving for this important need. Information on that opportunity is the mission of this chapter.

RETIREMENT HEALTHCARE FUNDING PLAN OVERVIEW

The NPPFA Retirement Healthcare Funding Plan (RHFP) was created in 2004. Today it has 110 separate entities participating, nearly 5500 individuals and $120 million in assets. The plan is administered under contract by NPPFA Benefits, professional benefit administrators.

The RHFP is a program for employers and both represented and non-represented labor interested in helping their employees and members deal with paying for the cost of health care and other related expenses in retirement. RHFP allows employees to pre-fund the future cost of health care expenses, including premiums, on a tax-exempt basis. Any form of compensation can be deposited into the plan, including the ability to shelter end of career payouts as a tax-exempt contribution.

Instead of spending your deferred compensation funds or a significant portion of your monthly pension check on insurance premiums, how would you like to pay for your medical expenses in retirement on a triple tax-free basis? This is possible. A Retirement Healthcare Funding Plan is a health care savings plan that provides a source of tax-free funds to reimburse participants for the cost of health care expenses for themselves, their spouses, and any other qualified tax-dependents.

What is the need?

There are many articles about the significant cost of health care in retirement. A 2020 Milliman study showed that a healthy 65-year-old couple should expect to incur $351,000 in medical costs while on Medicare between age 65 and death at 83 for the male and 85 for the female. The $351,000 amount does not include any long-term care needs, such as nursing home or in-home assistance.

Medical care costs are shown to increase 70% faster than general inflation. With the increasing reduction or absence of an employer subsidy for health care in retirement, many public sector workers are looking for solutions to allow them to pre-fund their retirement health care costs over their career on a tax-favorable basis.

Nearly all sworn fire and police retire prior to the age of 65. The below table represents the approximate dollars needed to pay for insurance premiums alone between the age of 55 and 65 (Medicare Eligibility).

Monthly Premium Today	**10-year Cost**
$800	$134,575
$1,000	$168,219
$1,250	$201,863
$1,500	$252,328
$2,000	$336,438

The above chart illustrates someone retiring at age 55 with health insurance premiums increasing 6.5% annually.

If someone retirees at age 55 with a monthly insurance premium of $1,250 today, they will incur on average $552,862 in premiums and out of pocket expense over the balance of their and their spouses' lives, not including any long-term care facility needs.

Tax advantages

The tax savings under Section 457 Deferred Compensation, either the traditional pre-tax or the Roth approach, are pretty impressive. But RHFP savings for future medical costs are even more supercharged for tax savings.

The plan provides triple-tax-free savings two times over. It's like the Chicago Bulls "three-peat." Which they did twice! *First*, there are elimination of federal, state and Social Security/Medicare taxes. For most of our members, that latter savings is just from Medicare (due to no participation in Social Security). But even without the Social Security savings, this tax break plus the magical value of compound earnings can make a substantial contribution towards reducing our membership's retiree medical expense.

And *second*, you pay no tax when the contribution is made, no tax on earnings while your money is invested, and, no tax on money drawn out.

No other retirement savings plan has these features. None.

Who can participate?

Participants by law must have an employment-related common bond. The most common is to be part of a defined unit for collective bargaining purposes (a union). But there are also non-union groups, and this can also include such groups as department heads, command staff, police and/or fire chief and potentially all employees. Once the group is defined, everyone participates, other than those who choose a one-time, lifetime opt out provision at the implementation of the plan. All future members are mandatorily covered.

So, this is different from Deferred Compensation. The rules on participation and how much is contributed are not individual choices. A participant's contribution is based upon a set of rules for that specific class of covered members.

How are contributions made?

Contributions are made in two ways. The first is a percentage of pay, most often in the 2% to 3% range. The second is via contribution of some or all accumulated leave either annually and/or at the time of retirement. But any form of compensation can be used. We have experience with some bargaining units agreeing *today* to new limits on accrued sick leave. Any amount over that new limit, on account now or earned in the future, is paid into the RHFP.

For the employees who contributes excess sick leave, they get the chance to begin investment growth on their earned leave *now* and capture that spectacular compound earnings math.

What should grow faster? Your investment account or increases in your wages? Your pay raises (averaging 3% and there are taxes due on your income) *versus* money that is in your RHFP which is completely tax exempt, including all of the growth and earnings? The S&P 500 Index has averaged approximately 10% over the past 90 years. *Do you want 10% tax-exempt growth or 3% taxable?*

For the city or fire district, it requires a payment today *but* the payment is made at today's salary and the sick leave obligation disappears from their required GASB financial statement disclosures.

PLAN CONTRIBUTION EXAMPLES

EXAMPLE #1

Every police union member contributes 40 hours of sick time pay annually. The City contributes $750 per year. At retirement, the police officer's unused sick and vacation time is cashed out and deposited into the Plan.

EXAMPLE #2

When a firefighter's sick bank accumulates over 400 hours, all hours over 400 are deposited into the Plan at 100% of value. Upon retirement, all accumulated sick day and vacation time is deposited into the Plan within 30 days of retirement.

EXAMPLE #3

Employees contribute 1% of salary and 100% of any end-of-career payout.

EXAMPLE #4

When the sick leave bank accumulates 318 hours to finish the year, all hours over 318 are deposited into the RHFP at 100% of value. At retirement, all accumulated sick day and vacation time is deposited into the RHFP within 30 days of retirement.

EXAMPLE #5

All employees pay a percentage of pay into the Plan on the following schedule:

Years of Service	Percent of Salary
0 – 2	0.0 %
3 – 7	1.5 %
8 – 15	3.0 %
Over 15	4.0 %

HOW IS THE MONEY INVESTED?

Investment decisions are individually employee driven; they choose from the same menu of funds, fixed return, or self-managed investments as are available in our companion 457 deferred compensation plan.

WHAT CAN THE MONEY BE USED FOR?

You can be reimbursed for all qualified medical expenses incurred after separation of service by you or any qualified tax dependent such as a spouse or child. Those expenses include:

- Insurance Premiums, including Medicare B, Medicare D, and Advantage or supplemental plans.
- Co-pays, including prescription drugs
- Deductibles
- Dental Costs
- Vision Costs
- Chiropractic
- Coinsurance
- Durable Medical Equipment (with doctor prescription)

We find that because each member has a finite amount of money, it is most efficient for them to file claims for insurance premiums which are large and easily substantiated as opposed to individual receipts for small balances due. That's not to say that a claimant can't come in with an envelope full of prescription drug copayment receipts! He or she can do so, but most don't.

Our administrator can count the number of claims denials on one hand—a claim for a non-dependent (a prescription drug for a dog), a hot tub without medical support, an elective cosmetic surgery, and a Peloton bike without medical support.

WHAT HAPPENS WHEN I DIE?

Payments at death are affected by the legal structure of the Plan. There are two legal approaches. A 501-c-9 Trust, sometimes called a VEBA (voluntary employee benefit association) has been allowable since 1928. Under a VEBA, there is no benefit or payment available to a non-tax dependent. If you die with an account balance and have a qualified dependent, your account is retitled in the dependent's name and they have immediate access to the funds for allowable expenses as if the member had separated service. *However,* if you die without a qualified dependent, the account is liquidated after any final claims are paid and the funds are distributed to the other active and retired participants in your group.

If your RHFP is set up under a 115 Trust (allowable since 1999), if you die with an account balance and have a qualified dependent, your account is retitled in the dependent's name and they have immediate access to the funds for allowable expenses as if the member had separated service. *However*, if you die without a qualified dependent, the account is liquidated after any final claims are paid and the funds are remitted to a beneficiary of your choice. This payment is taxable and the recipient will receive a 1099 tax form. Since tax is paid, these funds can be used for any purpose.

NPPFA Benefits will work with any public entity or employee unit to determine which legal structure is best for all parties.

SPECIAL ADVANTAGES FOR CITIES AND FIRE DISTRICTS

Cities and fire districts save the 1.45% match on all Medicare taxes avoided on contributions to the RHFP. If the employees are covered by Social Security, an additional 6.2% of pay is saved by the employer.

In addition to that calculable savings, employers also benefit when their workers don't delay retirement because they are unable to afford retiree medical costs. In an ideal world, all employees would start retirement at the optimum time. However, due to the rising costs of healthcare or inadequate retirement savings, many people simply cannot afford to stop working. This scenario impacts employers in terms of workforce resources and costs.

In a 2017 study using workforce composition and costs based on Illinois averages, an effort was made to quantify what the financial impact of delayed retirement takes on employers (See Prudential Financial: "Why employers should care above the cost of delayed retirement"). This study revealed that a one-year increase in average retirement age results in:

> An incremental cost of over $50,000 for an individual whose retirement is delayed. This represents the cost differential between the retiring employee and a newly hired employee.
>
> Incremental annual workforce costs of about 1.0%–1.5% for an entire workforce.

SUMMARY—ADVANTAGES OF RETIREMENT HEALTHCARE SAVINGS PLANS

Let's talk about two levels of value added. The first is that triple tax exemption. This is essentially free money—never taxed for federal/state/SSA/Medicare. And for the employer, they avoid the match on Medicare and, for some, Social Security. We are all going to have premiums and non-covered medical expenses in retirement. Why not reduce some of the cost by maybe 40% via tax breaks plus net asset growth?

The other value added is the opportunity to access these benefits via an association like the IPPFA. A newly formed fire department of three people can join in right alongside a still growing city with over 200 firefighters. Everything is all there—from the IRS Plan Determination Letter to the advisors to the 800-phone number to the internet access. This is available to our member plans throughout Illinois and the country.

CLOSING

The creation and operation of RHFP has given many individuals and their employer a reduction in costs to help both bridge the gap between our members' retirements and federal Medicare eligibility and then continue to reduce premium and other costs further into retirement.

IPPFA Benefits provides this plan on behalf of the Illinois Public Pension Fund Association (IPPFA). In an effort to improve the retirement outlook of the public sector employees that we serve, the IPPFA has paid for and made available a customizable and turn-key solution for each specific employer and/or bargaining unit.

CONTACTS:

NPPFA BENEFITS

Joel Babbitt, joelb@nppfabenefits.org, 773-617-9690

Anita Kochar, anitak@nppfabenefits.org, 847-323-0219

www.nppfabenefits.org

1701 E Lake Avenue Suite 400
Glenview, IL 60025

APPENDIX A

RETIREMENT HEALTHCARE FREQUENTLY ASKED QUESTIONS

Q. *What must I do to enroll in the plan?*

A. Your enrollment is automatic.

Q. *When can I access my funds?*

A. At separation of service. There is no age requirement.

Q. *For whose benefit can the funds be used?*

A. You and anyone you declare on your federal tax return as a dependent.

Q. *What can my funds be used for?*

A. Your funds may be used for anything deductible under IRC 213, which is the same code section that governs medical deductions on your federal income tax return. You may have a standing claim for all or part of your insurance premium that would produce a monthly reimbursement check, and you may submit claims for out-of-pocket expenses as incurred. Examples include physician and hospital charges, dental expenses, hearing and vision charges, prescriptions, ambulance services, laboratory fees, convalescent and nursing home care, hospice care, private nursing care, Medigap or Medicare supplement insurance premiums, other medical insurance premiums, deductibles or co-pay amounts, co-insurance costs, and other medical expenses that fall under Section 213 of the Internal Revenue Code.

Q. *What happens to my funds in the event of my death?*

A. Your surviving tax dependents have the same rights to the fund as before your death. If you have no surviving tax dependents, an NPPFA Benefits Representative can discuss your available options.

Q. *Are there set up charges?*

A. A $350 one-time charge payable to the NPPFA for documents needed to implement the plan is required. Two different types of trusts can be established; either a 501(c)(9) or a 115 trust. A 501(c)(9) trust requires a Letter of Determination (LOD) application with an additional one-time fee payable to the IRS. If an exemption for the annual tax return is not obtained, a 501(c)(9) trust requires that a tax return be prepared and is the responsibility of the plan sponsor. The establishment of at 115 trust requires no tax return and no separate IRS fee.

Q. *How are my funds invested?*

A. Our Retirement Healthcare Funding Plan uses a Transamerica Retirement Solutions investment platform. Investment options include twenty-two core asset class specific Vanguard indexes, five asset allocation funds, and a fixed stable/value fund without the typical liquidity restrictions. We also offer a Managed Account at no additional fee.

Q. *What are the administrative charges?*

A. All plan expenses are factored into the asset charges of the mutual funds. There are no participant expenses other than the investment related charges that currently range from 0.00% to 1.53% annually.

Q. *How do I file a claim for benefits?*

A. To obtain reimbursement for monthly insurance premiums or any other out of pocket medical expenses, simply complete the appropriate reimbursement form and submit to the plan administrator. All claims require corresponding proof of payment.

Q. *Is there sample union contract language?*

A. IPPFA Benefits can provide sample contract language to help establish your organization's Retirement Healthcare Funding Plan.

Q. *Who we are we?*

A. The Illinois Public Pension Fund Association (IPPFA) was founded by a small group of elected pension fund trustees as a not-for-profit umbrella organization representing police and fire defined benefit retirement funds in 1985. As the demand grew for prudent stewardship over governmental deferred compensation 457(b) plans, the IPPFA was established to offer low-cost benefit programs to the public sector employees in the state of Illinois.

NPPFA Benefits exclusively provides the Education, Sales, and Marketing for
the NPPFA 457(b) *Wise Choice for Public Employees* Plan,
the Retirement Healthcare Funding Plan,
and the *Wise Choice for Educators* 403(b)/457(b) Plan.

Appendix B

CONTRIBUTORS

Joel Babbitt, *NPPFA Benefits*
Joel J. Babbitt has been active in the insurance, investment, and Third-Party Administration business since 1987. Joel is the Benefit Coordinator for The Illinois Public Pension Fund Association (IPPFA) where he oversees the development and implementation of benefits programs for the jurisdictions represented by the member pension boards and others nationwide.

Allison Barrett, *Lauterbach & Amen, LLP.*
Since joining Lauterbach & Amen nearly 20 years ago, Allison has helped establish L&A's role as the recognized experts in Article 3 and Article 4 pension benefits administration. Ms. Barrett works with pension boards, pension fund members, the Illinois Department of Insurance, and the IRS to ensure the accuracy and timeliness of pension benefit calculations, payments, and reporting. Allison has developed instructional sections of the IPPFA Certified Trustee Program and Retirement Coordinator Program, and the IMTA Pension Administrator Certification Program, and is a frequent speaker at AFFI, IAFPD, IGFOA, IMTA, IPFA, IPPFA, and NIAFPD events.

James McNamee, *IPPFA*
Born in Chicago, Jim McNamee began his career in law enforcement in 1979 as a police officer for the Village of Barrington. In 1983, Mr. McNamee was elected to the Barrington Police Pension Board as a trustee. During his term as trustee, he quickly saw the need for training and education for all trustees of pension boards. Taking action, Mr. McNamee went to work to form the Illinois Police Pension Fund Association now known as the Illinois Public Pension Fund Association.

Daniel W. Ryan, *Retired*
Dan is retired from careers as a municipal finance director and union benefit administrator and is a longtime trustee of the Skokie police pension fund. His research and writings on Social Security and public pensions have been referenced in pension fund newsletters and newspapers nationwide. He is a part-time project coordinator for IPPFA.

IPPFA Association Office
Administrative assistance was provided by IPPFA office staff Julie Guy, Mandy Paciorkowski and Madeline Lusted.

Appendix C

"HELPS" Tax Break Retiree Medical Insurance Payments

Retired police and firefighters/EMTs may be able to reduce their taxable earnings by up to $3,000 for medical insurance premiums paid during a calendar year. This is allowable under the Healthcare Enhancement for Local Public Safety Retirees Act, or the "HELPS" Retiree Act.

When initially passed, there was a requirement that the premium be deducted from the retiree's pension check in order to qualify for HELPS tax break. That is no longer the case following the adoption of the federal Secure 2.0 retirement law. Premiums paid directly to the insurer for health, accident, or long-term care insurance qualify for the credit. Note that the tax break is not available to surviving spouses.

The $3,000 reduction does not appear on the 1099R form from the pension fund. The retiree must claim the reduction on his or her personal 1040 tax form on Line 5B or similar adjustment. Instructions on claiming the reduction are included in IRS Publication 575, page 7 with update on page 2. As this is not a simple matter, you may want to consult with a tax preparer to properly claim the reduction.

Note that married couples where both the parties are retired police/fire/EMS may take a reduction in income of up to $6,000.

More information on this subject is available at IPPFA.org.
Click on Bulletins, then select the HELPS Retiree Insurance Bulletin.